POLE VAULT

Becca Jones

CW01082952

by Peter Sutcliffe
(Technical Adviser on Pole Vault, U.K. Coaching Scheme)

First published 1954 (by Denis Watts)
Revised Edition 1960 (by Denis Watts)
Second Edition 1962 (by Ian Ward)
Third Edition 1966 (by Ian Ward)
Fourth Edition 1975 (by Alan Neuff)
This Edition 1991 (by Peter Sutcliffe)

ISBN 0 85134 100 4   2M/27M/03/91

© British Amateur Athletic Board
Edgbaston House, 3 Duchess Place, Birmingham B16 8NM

ABOUT THE AUTHOR

A graduate of the University of Leeds, Peter Sutcliffe is Deputy Headmaster of Hounslow College. He began coaching pole vault in 1970 and was Event Coach for the Southern Counties A.A. 1979-82. He served as National Event Coach 1982-89 and is now the B.A.A.B.'s Technical Adviser for this event. He has acted as Team Coach to a number of international teams and the athletes he has coached include Andrew Ashurst, the 1986 Commonwealth Pole Vault Champion. Peter has also worked in schools athletics as coach and administrator for many years and is a member of his local Sports Council.

ACKNOWLEDGMENTS

My thanks are due to all those coaches and athletes with whom I have had contact since I began coaching pole vault. In particular I wish to thank:

Dr. M. Lindsay and Dr. J. Bryant, both of the Department of Physical Education of the University of Leeds, and Peter Warden (National Coach).

I am also grateful for the use of the following illustrations:

Cover photo of Kory Tarpenning (USA) by Dr. Howard Payne
Photo sequence of Thierry Vigneron (France) by Helmar Hommel
Other photo sequences and photo by Dr. Howard Payne
Drawings by Justin Richards and Ernie Williams

Peter Sutcliffe

Designed, typeset in Times Roman and printed on 115 gsm Fineblade Cartridge by Reedprint Limited, Windsor, Berkshire, England.

CONTENTS

HISTORY OF THE POLE VAULT

EARLY HISTORY

The use of a pole as an aid to jumping dates back to antiquity and a variety of historical sources indicate that some form of pole leaping was in existence from the 5th century BC until the 17th century. However, vaulting in these early days was probably confined to vaulting for distance and there is no real evidence of vaulting for height as a proper competitive event.

A description of pole vaulting in the modern sense first appears in Gutsmuths' book "Gymnastik für die Jugend", published in 1793, but true competitive vaulting almost certainly started in England in the Lake District town of Ulverston. The annual sports meeting at Flan, near Ulverston, was first held in 1834 and the 'Ulverston Advertiser' in 1849 reports that:

> "An addition that appeared particularly attractive was made to the leaping prizes. It showed the daring and agile manner in which the youth of the district can, with the assistance of a pole, clear at one bound a bar between eight and nine feet high."[1]

In these early days of organized athletics the world's finest pole-vaulters came from Ulverston and using the pole climbing technique in 1881 Tom Ray of the local cricket club set a world's best performance of 11 feet and 3 inches.

Within a few years however the climbing technique was banned (in 1889 in the U.S.A. and 1919 in Britain) and this together with the change from the ash or hickory pole to bamboo paved the way for the dominance of the event by the U.S.A.

The Bamboo Era (1900-1948)

Although the Bamboo Era was dominated by the American vaulters it was in fact a Norwegian who popularized the event and brought it to the attention of the public.

Charlie Hoff can lay claim to be one of the greatest all round athletes of all time. Between 1922 and 1925 he set 4 world records in the pole vault (recording 10 Indoor World Records) and set personal bests for the 100m., 10.8; 200m., 21.9; 400m., 49.2; 800m., 1.55.9; high hurdles, 15.2; triple jump, 14.38m.

The 'King of the Bamboo Pole' was however an American, Cornelius 'Dutch' Warmerdam, who despite never winning an Olympic title (largely as a result of the Second World War) became in 1940 the first vaulter to scale the 15 feet barrier, a feat no other vaulter was to achieve until 1951. Warmerdam went on to clear 15 feet 43 times and broke his own world indoor and outdoor records on eight different occasions.

The Metal Era (1948-1960)

The introduction of alloy and steel poles in no way affected the domination of the event by the Americans. Bob Richards was the legendary pole vaulter of this era. Although he was unable ever to better Warmerdan's world record — this was finally achieved by Bob Gutouski in 1957 — Bob Richards is the

---

[1] I. Ward, Pole Vaulting, A.A.A., 1966, p.5.

1

only man in history to win two Olympic Pole Vault titles and in his career vaulted over fifteen feet more than 140 times.[2] The metal pole however was destined to have a relatively short international life. Although Don Bragg won the 1960 Olympic title on a metal pole, the advent of the fibreglass pole was to change the event for ever.

The Age of Fibreglass

Although the fibreglass pole was first used as early as 1948[3], it was not until the 1960s that it really came into its own. As was to be expected, the Americans continued to dominate the event and between 1963 and 1969 the world record was bettered 21 times (although some marks were not officially ratified), and was raised from 4.94m. to 5.44m. Three great American vaulters were to dominate the sixties: John Pennel, nine times world record holder; Fred Hansen who broke the world record on three occasions and won the 1964 Olympic title; and Bob Seagren who broke the world record six times and was the winner of the 1968 Olympic title.

By 1969 the American domination of the event was beginning to wane. Europe was about to launch an assault on the event. In 1970 Wolfgang Nordwig (G.D.R.) set a new world record of 5.45m. and with his victory in the 1972 Olympic Games established himself as one of the greatest technicians in the history of the event. Europeans continued to 'infiltrate' the event at the highest level. A little known Greek vaulter by the name of Chris Papanicolaou became the first man to reach the 'magic' height of 18 feet in 1970 and in the following year Kjell Isaksson of Sweden began an assault on the world record which was to establish him as one of Europe's greatest ever vaulters.

The Americans retaliated with vaulters of the calibre of Dave Roberts and Earl Bell, both of whom were to set world records, but the emergence of new European vaulters from Poland (Buciarski, Slusarski, Kozakiewicz) and France (Asada and Bellot) indicated that American domination of the event was at an end.

More recently the pendulum has swung even further in favour of the Europeans. France, with vaulters of the calibre of Houvion, Vigneron, Quiñon and Collet has shown that it can challenge the best, while the exploits of Soviet Union vaulters such as Bubka and Gataullin suggest that it could be some time before the Americans can seriously challenge European supremacy.

---

[2] Dr. R.V. Gansten, Mechanics of the Pole Vault, 9th Edition, 1979.

[3] Dr. R.V. Gansten, Mechanics of the Pole Vault, 7th Edition, 1970.

POLE VAULT RULES

The following extracts are printed from the A.A.A. rules for competition (1990/91 edition).

GENERAL CONDITIONS

Rule 41 (Time allotted for making a jump).

Two minutes, the time beginning as soon as the uprights have been adjusted to the satisfaction of the competitor. When three or fewer competitors remain in the competition, the time should be extended to four minutes.

Rule 42

1. Unless such details are specified in the programme, the judge shall decide the height at which the competition shall start, and the different heights to which the bar will be raised at the end of each round. The competitors shall be informed of the details before the competition begins.

2. Competitors may commence vaulting at any of the heights above the minimum height and may vault at their own discretion at any subsequent height. Three consecutive failures, regardless of the height at which any such failure occurs, disqualify from further participation, except in the case of a jump-off of a first place tie.

   NOTE: The effect of this Rule is that competitors may forego their second and third vaults at a particular height (after failing once or twice) and still vault at a subsequent height. If competitors forego a trial at a certain height, they may not make any subsequent attempt at that height except in the resolution of a tie.

3. Even after all the other competitors have failed, a competitor is entitled to continue until he or she has forfeited the right to compete further, and the best vault shall be recorded as the winning height.

4. After the competitor has won the competition the height or heights to which the bar is raised shall be decided after the judge or referee in charge of the event has consulted the wishes of the competitor.

   NOTE: This does not apply for Combined Events competitions.

5. All measurements shall be made perpendicularly from the ground to the upper side of the cross-bar where it is lowest. A steel or fibre-glass measure should be used.

6. (a) The height shall be recorded to the nearest 1cm. below the height measured if that distance is not a whole centimetre.

   (b) Unless there is only one competitor remaining the bar shall not be raised by less than 5cms. after each round.

7. Ties
   Ties shall be decided as follows:

   (a) The competitor with the lowest number of vaults at the height at which the tie occurs shall be awarded the higher place.

   (b) If the tie still remains, the competitor with the lowest total of failures throughout the competition up to and including the height last cleared shall be awarded the higher place.

(c) If the tie still remains:

   (i) if it concerns first place, the competitors tying shall have one more vault at the lowest height at which any of them finally failed, and if no decision is reached the bar shall be lowered or raised 5cms. They shall then attempt one vault at each height until one competitor clears a height and the remaining competitor(s) fail at the same height. Competitors so tying must vault on each occasion when resolving the tie.

   (ii) if it concerns any other place, the competitors shall be awarded the same place in the competition.

Rule 45

1. No marks may be placed on the runways, but a competitor may place marks alongside the runway.

2. The distance of the run-up is unlimited.

3. Competitors may have the uprights moved in either direction, but not more than 40cms. in the direction of the runway, and not more than 80cms. to the landing area from the prolongation of the inside edge of the top of the box.

4. The take-off for the pole shall be from a wooden or metal box. A competitor is permitted to place sand in the box when it is his turn to vault.

5. A competitor fails if he:

  (a) in the course of a vault dislodges the bar so that it falls from the pegs; or

  (b) touches the ground, including the landing area beyond the vertical plane of the upper part of the box with any part of his body or with the pole, without first clearing the bar; or

  (c) at the moment he makes a vault, or after leaving the ground, places his lower hand above the upper one, or moves the upper hand higher up on the pole.

6. No one should touch the pole unless it is falling away from the bar or uprights; if it is so touched and the referee or judge is of the opinion it would have dislodged the bar so that it fell from the pegs the vault shall be recorded as a failure.

7. Competitors may use their own poles. No competitor shall be allowed to use another's pole except with the consent of the owner.

8. The pole may be of any material or combination of materials and any length or diameter, but the basic surface must be smooth. The pole may have a binding of not more than two layers of adhesive tape of uniform thickness and with a smooth surface. The pole shall have no other assistance or device, except that the lower end of the pole may have protective layers of tape for a distance of approximately 30cms.

9. The use of tape on the hands or fingers shall not be allowed except in the case of need to cover an open cut. The use of a forearm cover to prevent

injury shall be allowed. Competitors are permitted to use an adhesive substance on their hands or on the pole, in order to obtain a better grip.

10. If in making an attempt the competitor's pole is broken it shall not be counted as a failure.

N.B. For Pole Vault Specifications see **Rule 46**.

For competitions held under I.A.A.F. rules, vaulters and coaches should note the following differences from A.A.A.'s rules.

1. **Delays** — the following times should not normally be exceeded.

   (a) Two minutes for the pole vault. The time shall begin when the uprights have been adjusted according to the previous wishes of the competitor.

The effect of this rule is that the officials will adjust the standards for a competitor immediately after the completion of the previous vault. Any change made after the officials have set the standards will be in the competitor's time.

   (b) In the final stages of competition (but not in a Combined Events competition), when only 2 or 3 competitors continue in the competition, the above time should be increased to 4 minutes. If there is only one competitor left, this time should be increased to 6 minutes.

   (c) The period between two consecutive trials by the same athlete should never be less than 4 minutes.

2. **Assistance**

   For the purposes of this rule the following shall *not* be considered as assistance:

   Verbal or other communication, without the use of any technical device, from an individual who is not in the competition area.

   For further details see the I.A.A.F. Handbook.

SAFETY

Coaches, officials and administrators have a moral and legal duty to ensure that vaulting takes place in a safe environment.

Pole vaulting is a safe activity provided certain precautions are taken:

LANDING AREAS (see Fig. 1)

(a) A safe landing area must be provided. The size of the landing area must be compatible with the standard of the vaulters using it. For vaulters of county, area or international standard, i.e. jumping approximately 4.00m. or higher, a landing area measuring 7.12m. × 6.50m. with a thickness of 0.80m. is suitable. In training under the supervision of an experienced coach an area measuring 5.00m. × 6.30m. would be adequate.

(b) The area immediately around the box must be adequately protected. The shape of the cut-out section of the landing area should be such as to allow for the bending of the pole but close enough to the edge of the box to protect the vaulter.

(c) Landing areas should be inspected regularly for gaps and holes. Foam in older areas often deteriorates and the section may become difficult to keep together. A wear sheet must be used at all times.

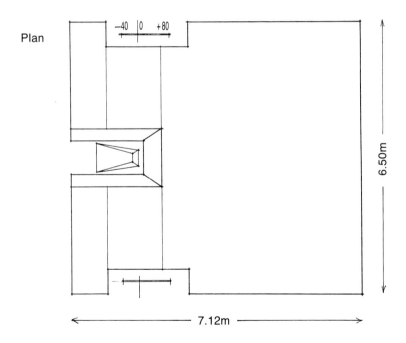

Fig. 1 A Pole Vault Landing Area suitable for International Competition

Fig. 1 continued

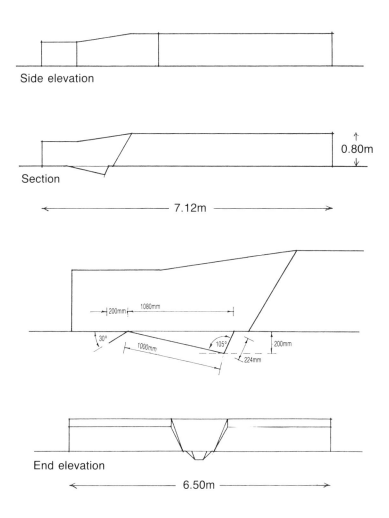

Side elevation

Section

0.80m

7.12m

200mm 1080mm

30° 1000mm

105° 200mm

224mm

End elevation

6.50m

THE RUNWAY

(a) Should not have protruding edges.

(b) Care must be taken to ensure that the take-off point does not become too worn.

STANDS

Must be firmly secured. Particular care should be taken if an elastic bar is being used in training.

THE BOX
Must conform to A.A.A. specifications and should be immovable with the front lip completely flush with the surface of the runway.

BAR
Bars with triangular cross-section should not be used.

THE SURROUNDS
The area around the landing area should be free of any dangerous projections. UNDER NO CIRCUMSTANCES SHOULD THE GROUND IN THE VICINITY OF THE LANDING AREA BE COVERED IN CONCRETE, TARMAC OR ANY SIMILAR SUBSTANCE.

THE WEATHER
Vaulting will not always take place in the most favourable weather conditions but heavy rain or adverse winds can make the event hazardous. Due consideration must always be given to the skill and experience of the vaulter concerned and to the nature of the competition. As a general rule vaulters should not compete into headwinds, and they should only be allowed to do so if the heights they are attempting and their experience are such that coaches deem that it is safe.

VAULTING POLES

Fibreglass vaulting poles are manufactured in various lengths and stiffnesses. The flexibility of a pole is measured by the weight of the vaulter it is designed to carry and in consequence a vaulter will make use of many different poles in the course of his vaulting career.

BEGINNERS' POLES

These include the English made Bantex poles which range from 50 lbs. 11 feet long to 150 lbs. 15 feet long. These poles are durable and relatively inexpensive but the longer poles are rather heavy. A lighter pole is the Bantex Alpha which is suitable for 85 lbs. bodyweight.

Rather more expensive are several ranges of American poles: Pacer, Spirit, Skypole, Nordic and Cata-pole Gam poles. These poles range from 10 feet to 13 feet and cater for a variety of bodyweights from 65 lbs. upwards.

TRAINING POLES

A number of poles exist primarily for training purposes. These poles are very strong and durable. They bend more easily than competition poles and recoil more slowly. They are designed to improve technique and have a wide bodyweight range. The most popular of these types of pole are the French Lerc Initiation Poles, the American Cata-pole Training Poles and the American Fibersport Training Poles.

COMPETITION POLES

A wide variety of competition poles is available ranging in length from 10 feet to 17 feet and catering for bodyweights between 65 lbs and 220 lbs. The most widely available today are the Catapole Gold ''MX'' Series poles; Pacer poles; Spirit poles; Skypole poles; Nordic poles; Fibersport Fiberflex Competition II and Competition III poles and Fibersport High Performance Maxima 4 poles.

A vaulter should choose a pole suited to his physique, ability and technique. Many variations exist among these poles ranging from the present 'banana' poles such as the 'Banana' Skypole to the carbon fibre poles of Nordic. Some poles such as the Fibersport and Fiberflex Competition poles are more suited to vaulters who jump 4m. or below while others such as Catapole, Skypole, Pacer and Spirit can claim many world records set using their poles.

POLE SELECTION

The Beginner

As poles come in a variety of sizes a vaulter must select a pole which suits his own requirements. The most important considerations are the weight of the vaulter and his handhold, although the technical expertise of the vaulter will also play a part. A vaulter should choose a pole which corresponds to his bodyweight and his handhold. Thus a vaulter who weighs 120 lbs. and has an effective grip of 13 feet will select a 14 feet 120 lbs. pole, whereas a vaulter who weighs 150 lbs. and has a grip of 14 feet will select a 15 feet

150 lbs. pole. This presupposes that a pole is being held close to its end. A lower grip will make a pole less easy to bend — a grip one foot lower on a pole approximates to adding 10 lbs. to the rated strength of the pole. It is important therefore that a vaulter should have a handhold appropriate to his ability. As a rough guide one would expect a beginner aged 12-13 years to use a pole 10-11 feet long, aged 14-15 13 feet long, aged 16-17 years 14 feet long, and 18 years onwards 14 or 15 feet long.

The Top-Class Performer

The needs of a top-class performer will be somewhat different to those of a novice. International vaulters require poles tailor-made to their own requirements, and vaulters of this standard will use poles rated well in excess of their bodyweight. Slight variations in the flexibility of a pole can make significant differences to vaulters of this standard and in consequence the *flex* of a pole becomes critical.

All poles are tested by manufacturers for flexibility by suspending a weight from the centre of the pole and measuring the amount the pole bends. This distance, measured in centimetres or inches, represents *the flex* of the pole and the rated poundage of a pole will correspond to a range of flex numbers. While poles are sold in ranges of 5 or 10 lbs. the flex number of a pole will differ by as little as 1 lb. Thus an international vaulter will be able to find a pole totally suited to his needs. Additionally poles vary in their circumference and vaulters may require a pole of a certain 'mandril'.

The Club Situation

A club's problems in purchasing poles are slightly different to those of the individual vaulter in that it has to satisfy the needs of existing vaulters but also be able to supply poles for newcomers to the event. Unless a club can maintain a complete range of poles a suitable selection for young vaulters might be as follows:

11 ft. 6 ins.	100 lbs.	13 ft.	120 lbs.	14 ft.	135 lbs.	15 ft.	150 lbs.
		13 ft.	130 lbs.	14 ft.	145 lbs.		
				14 ft.	155 lbs.		

If a club wishes to cater more for its senior members then the selection might be:

14 ft.	150 lbs.	15 ft.	155 lbs.	15 ft. 9 ins.	165 lbs.
14 ft.	160 lbs.	15 ft.	165 lbs.	15 ft. 9 ins.	175 lbs.

It is a short-sighted policy to buy a single pole or even two poles and allow all vaulters to use them. Not only will they be unsuitable for most of the vaulters, but excessive use will inevitably shorten their life. If they are looked after correctly fibreglass poles will last for many years.

CARE OF FIBREGLASS POLES

Fibreglass poles are very resilient but will break if they are ill-treated. Many breakages can be avoided if vaulters follow a few simple rules:

(a) Every pole has what is known as a 'preferred' bend. That is, every pole will bend more easily in one direction than in any other. Any attempt to bend the pole in another direction can damage the pole and cause injury to the vaulter. To find the preferred bend, place one end of the pole on a hurdle with the other end resting on the ground. Rotate the pole until it comes to rest in the same position each time. The bend of the pole will be in the direction of the ground.

(b) Vaulters should not use poles that are too soft for them. As a general rule a pole should not be bent more than 90 degrees and for most vaulters gripping below the end of the pole, the bend should be considerably less than this. In addition vaulters who pull down on a pole immediately after take-off are liable to overbend a pole.

(c) Poles should not be bent in the box for practice.

(d) If a vaulter does not take off and runs through the landing area, he must be careful not to allow his pole to hit the crossbar, or uprights, nor let the end of the pole wedge itself under the landing area (a not uncommon occurrence if the landing area is slightly raised off the ground). Beware of the winders on standards and do not allow poles to fall onto the ground after a vault. Vaulters should be encouraged to catch each others poles. When not in use poles should not be left lying on the ground where they are liable to be damaged by athletes' spikes.

(e) Poles need to be regularly checked for damage. It is inevitable that they will become scratched, but provided that there are no deep cuts the pole will be safe to use. If the ends of a pole are damaged they may be sawn off. However it should be remembered that (i) if a pole is shortened at the handgrip end the bending characteristics of the pole will be changed, and (ii) as the lower end of the pole is specially strengthened it could be dangerous to cut off anything more than one or two centimetres there. To protect the end of a pole from being damaged by the back of the box a pole should be taped for the bottom 30 centimetres.

(f) To assist the vaulter to grip the pole the rules allow a binding of not more than two layers of tape of uniform thickness. In addition vaulters often use an adhesive substance on their tape or on their hands. The most common substance used is lighter fuel but resin (as used for musical instruments) or resin mixed with turpentine is very effective.

(g) At regular intervals check the condition of the pole tip and if necessary replace it. If rubber tips are being used ensure that the edges at the end of the pole are smooth and not jagged.

MECHANICS OF THE POLE VAULT

Mechanics is an area which often frightens coaches, but a basic knowledge of the mechanics of pole vaulting is essential for every coach of the event at every level.

A. WHAT THE COACH NEEDS TO KNOW — THE BASIC PRINCIPLES.[1]

1. **Momentum** = mass × velocity.

Linear momentum, i.e. momentum in a straight line, is primarily achieved by the vaulter in his approach.

Angular momentum, i.e. momentum around a fixed point, is achieved by the vaulter after take-off. The conservation of angular momentum is a key factor in a good vault and is achieved by a combination of the physical and technical qualities of the vaulter.

2. **Energy** = the capacity to do work.

Kinetic energy, i.e. energy achieved by virtue of an athlete's motion, is present during a vaulter's approach, take-off, swing and extension.

Potential energy, i.e. the energy a body has by virtue of its position, is stored in the fibreglass pole when it is bent and is restored to the vaulter as it straightens.

3. **Centre of Gravity** = the point at which all the mass of an object is concentrated. The position of the vaulter's centre of gravity during the vault is critical to a successful vault. A change in the position of the centre of gravity of the vaulter on the pole will either increase or decrease the vaulter's angular momentum and affect the forward momentum of the pole.

4. **Moment of Inertia** = the distribution of mass about an axis. The closer the mass is to the axis the faster the mass will rotate. In the pole vault there are two axis points — the vaulter's handgrip on the pole and the pole in the vaulting box (the double pendulum). The closer the mass of the vaulter is to his handhold, the faster the vaulter will rotate, whereas by lowering his mass the rotational speed of the pole is increased.

B. THE RELATIONSHIP BETWEEN MECHANICAL PRINCIPLES AND THE VAULT

1. **The Benefits of a Fibreglass Pole**

A fibreglass pole enables a vaulter to vault higher for the following reasons:

(a) It enables a vaulter to use a higher grip. By bending, the fibreglass pole increases the angle between the pole and the ground at take-off and makes it easier for the vaulter to get the pole upright.

(b) By bending, the pole stores kinetic energy which is released when the pole straightens. For this reason the vaulter should use as stiff a pole as possible.

---

[1] For a more detailed explanation refer to the B.A.A.B. Senior Coach Award Theory Manual.

The stiffer the pole the faster will be the recoil and the greater will be the advantage to the vaulter.

2. Factors that affect the vaulter's handhold on the pole

A vaulter's handhold on the pole will vary considerably, the best vaulters using an effective grip of 5 metres (the length of the pole less 20 cms. for the depth of the vaulting box).

A vaulter's handhold will be determined by the following factors: his height, technique, speed and jumping power, the direction and strength of the wind and his courage and determination.

3. The Approach

The close correlation between the vaulter's speed and the height achieved is not a disputed fact. Using the formula $\frac{1}{2}mv^2 = mgh$ where:

m = the mass of the vaulter
g = acceleration due to gravity
v = the vaulter's velocity
h = the height cleared

Dyson in 'Mechanics of Athletics' has shown that all other things being equal, the height cleared in pole vaulting is proportional to the square of the take-off velocity.

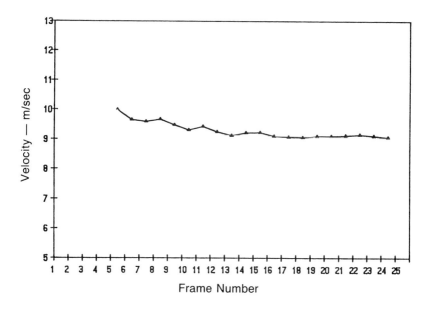

Fig. 2 Velocity profile of Keith Stock (G.B.) 2 strides from take-off to take-off. (Frame 25 indicates take-off point)

---

[1] G. Dyson, 'Mechanics of Athletics', Hodder & Stoughton, 8th Edition, 1986, p.196.

13

Ideally there should be a gradual build-up of speed with the minimum loss of speed over the last strides to take-off. In reality, as Fig. 2 showing velocity losses at take-off indicates, even international vaulters find it difficult to maintain their acceleration into take-off.

4. The Plant and Take-off

The purpose of the plant is to place the pole in the most suitable position for converting kinetic energy into potential energy, for converting linear to angular momentum and to move the pole to a vertical position. In order to achieve this the vaulter must drive the pole forwards and upwards, and plant as high as possible.

5. The Hang and Swing

To assist penetration the vaulter will momentarily delay his swing keeping his take-off leg extended. The free leg will generally remain flexed, driving forwards and upwards. Any lowering of this leg will assist penetration, though at the expense of the vaulter's angular momentum. During this phase the vaulter must continue to drive the pole forwards with his arms.

Fig. 3 illustrates that if the pole is to continue to move forward and achieve the penetration necessary to reach the vertical, the pole must rotate around point X. To achieve this the resultant force of the vaulter on the pole represented by AD must be directed beyond point X.

AB = Vaulter's horizontal force
AC = Vaulter's vertical force
RD = Resultant force.

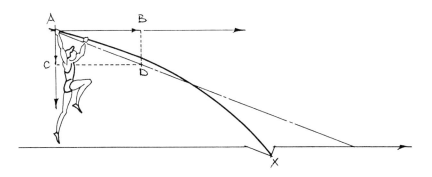

Fig. 3

From an extended position the vaulter must raise his centre of gravity as quickly as possible in order to conserve his angular momentum and be in a position to benefit from the recoil of the pole.

6. The Rock Back

The vaulter should reach the rock back position by the time the pole reaches maximum bend. As Fig. 4 shows, at that time the forward drive of the vaulter

14

is severely limited and the vaulter must aim at raising his hips as quickly as possible. Those vaulters who tuck tightly require a vigorous extension of the hips and legs up the pole, while those who assume a pronounced pike position must ensure that they have sufficient penetration to be able to cover the arc of the pole with the legs (see Fig. 5).

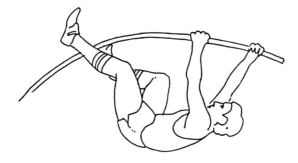

Fig. 4 The rock back position

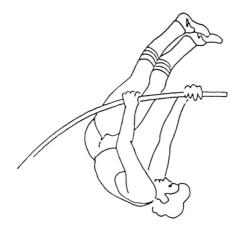

Fig. 5 Vaulter covering the arc of the pole with his legs

7. The Extension

If the vaulter has achieved a correct position close to the pole during the extension phase, the recoil of the pole will add to the vaulter's momentum thereby giving him the appearance of exploding off the top of his pole. Consequently, provided he has sufficient penetration, the vaulter should be in a position to execute an extension before the pole straightens. The earlier he achieves this

15

position the more benefit he will gain from the pole. For this reason the vaulter should use as stiff a pole as he is able to bend and control effectively.

During the extension phase the vaulter will pull and turn as the pole recoils. The direction the vaulter will take is determined by the closeness of his hips and legs to the pole; any deviation from the pole will result in the vaulter losing momentum and 'flattening out' towards the bar.

8. Bar Clearance

The bar clearance is to a large extent determined by the rest of the vault; however the position adopted over the bar affects the vaulter's centre of gravity.

The jack-knife position (Fig. 43 on p.40) allows the vaulter to raise his body above his centre of gravity.

The flyaway position (Fig. 42 on p.40) is only effective if arms and legs are thrown back together.

TEACHING THE BEGINNER

Teaching the beginner to vault can be approached in five stages. The duration of each stage will to a large extent depend upon the age and ability of each individual athlete. These stages are:

(a) Introduction on the ground
(b) Vault into sand
(c) Introduction to a landing area
(d) Full approach and vault into a landing area
(e) Bending the pole.

STAGE ONE

This can be performed on the ground and consists of a swing on the pole from a single stride approach. The surface should be non-slip and can be grass or a running track.

The Grip

For a right-handed vaulter the top (upper) hand will be the right hand, and for left-handed vaulters the top hand will be the left hand. Holding the pole parallel to the ground, the athlete should grasp the pole with the lower hand palm down and the top hand palm upwards. The hands should be approximately shoulder width apart and the top hand should be at about head height on the pole (Figs. 6a, 6b and 7).

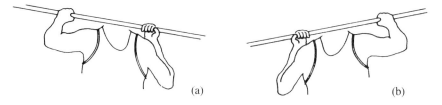

Fig. 6 The grip (a) right handed vaulter, (b) left handed vaulter

Fig. 7 The position of the upper hand on the pole

17

The Carry and Swing *(note that instructions are for right-handed vaulters)*
Carrying the pole on the right side of the body, the athlete steps forward, places the top of the pole on the ground in front of him and, placing his left foot as close as possible to the bottom of the pole and keeping his top hand as high as possible, takes off from the *left* foot, drives the right knee forward, passes the pole on the *right* side, turns and lands on both feet facing the opposite direction to the one he took off from, still holding the pole with both hands (Fig. 8).

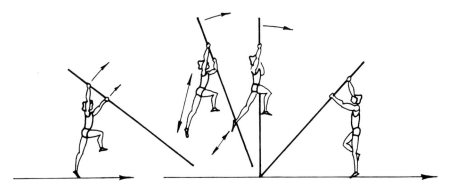

Fig. 8 The swing

Points to note:
(a) Right-handed vaulters *must* take-off from the *left* foot. Left-handed vaulters *must* take-off from the *right* foot.
(b) Right-handed vaulters pass the pole on the right side.
(c) The top arm must be kept straight.

NOTE: The turn, which is often ignored at this stage, makes this manoeuvre much easier to perform. Without it there is often a tendency for the athlete to overbalance.

This exercise should be repeated until the athlete is fully confident and has a balanced take-off and landing.

STAGE TWO
Vault into Sand (Fig. 9)
A similar procedure to that adopted in Stage One is followed in Stage Two, except that the top of the pole is planted in a sand pit. The athlete is now able to raise his handgrip gradually and increase his approach to 4-6 strides. During this stage the coach must ensure that the pole is planted in front of the athlete and that the top arm remains high and straight at take-off. The athlete should first vault for distance and then for height. Only when the athlete can consistently lift both legs higher than 90 cms. and land well into the sand should he progress to the next stage. If necessary an elastic bar can be stretched across the pit to encourage the athlete to raise his legs into the air.

18

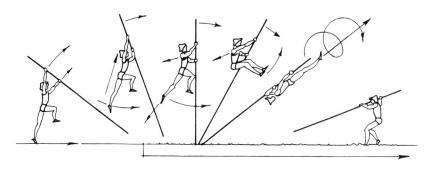

Fig. 9 The vault into sand

STAGE THREE
Introduction to a Landing Area

As soon as the athlete is able to progress to using a proper landing area, the approach run can be increased to 6-8 strides and the handgrip raised. At this stage more attention needs to be paid to the grip and plant.

The Grip

The vaulter should grip the pole with the right (top) arm bent at right angles, holding the pole at the right hip with the pole resting between the fingers and thumb. The left arm should be flexed at 90° with the left hand grasping the pole palm down. The tip of the pole should be held at approximately head height.

Fig. 10 The grip and carry

The Plant

The plant refers to the act of placing the bottom of the pole into the pole vault box in preparation for taking off. In fibreglass vaulting the plant must be fast, high and early. The plant action should begin two strides from take-off when the vaulter's left foot (for a right-handed vaulter) touches the ground. The plant is initiated by moving both arms forwards and upwards. The right (upper) arm should be in a vertical position before the bottom of the pole hits the

19

back of the box and the plant action should be completed as soon as the left foot touches the ground (see Fig. 37 on p.35).

STAGE FOUR
Full Approach and Vault into Landing Area
The Approach

A measured approach of 10-12 strides is now required and the coach must ensure that the vaulter takes off from the correct position. The take-off point can be determined by placing the bottom of the pole in the box with the vaulter positioning himself so that his top arm is fully extended vertically and the take-off foot is placed directly beneath the top hand. The position of the take-off foot marks the take-off position (Fig. 11).

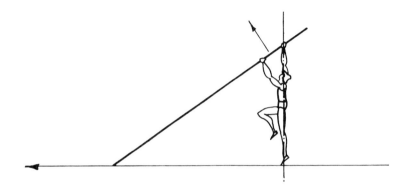

Fig. 11 Take-off position

The Plant

The plant action needs constant practice since bad habits acquired at this stage tend to be difficult to eradicate later. In particular, care should be taken to ensure that during the plant the top hand keeps close to the body and a 'round arm' action is avoided (Figs. 12a & b).

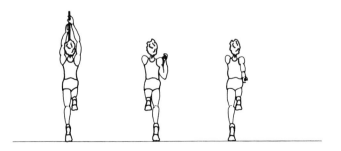

Fig. 12a The plant from behind (right handed vaulter)

20

Fig. 12b The plant from behind (left handed vaulter)

Take-off

The take-off should be vigorous (similar to a long jump take-off), with the free knee driven forcibly upwards.

The Swing

After the take-off the vaulter must learn to swing the take-off leg, bring both legs into a tucked position, turn and clear a bar, pushing the pole away with the top hand (Fig. 13).

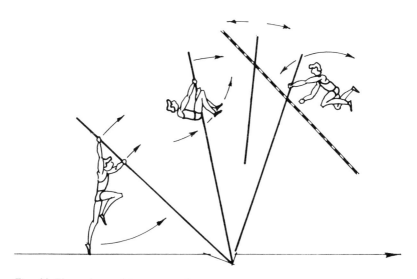

Fig. 13 The swing and turn over a bar

STAGE 5

Bending the Pole

When the vaulter has mastered the technique in Stage Four he can progress to bending the pole. It is important to realise that bending the pole should

21

be a natural progression from the previous stages, and should not be taught until the athlete has learnt to swing correctly. This stage should only be attempted under the supervision of an experienced coach, and is dependent upon the vaulter possessing the correct fibreglass pole (see Chapter headed "Vaulting Poles").

Learning to Bend the Pole

Bending the fibreglass pole should be the natural consequence of a correct handhold on a suitably sized pole. A grip which is too low on a pole, or a pole which is too stiff, will make it difficult if not impossible for the vaulter to bend the pole. To assist the bend, the vaulter should attempt to keep the body away from the pole at and immediately after take-off, using the lower arm (Fig. 14).

Fig. 14 Bending the pole

If the athlete has difficulty in accomplishing this, he may find it easier using a shortened approach, or simply jumping from a box into a sand pit (Fig. 15).

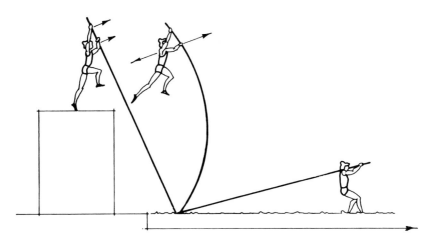

Fig. 15 Vaulting from a box into sand

Once the pole begins to bend, the vaulter must ensure that the bend is towards the left-hand corner of the box (right-hand corner for a left-handed vaulter). To achieve this the vaulter should grip the pole with the preferred bend of the pole facing the ground, then slightly rotate the pole in an anti-clockwise direction. The pole will then be in a correct position at take-off.

N.B. To find the preferred bend of the pole see 'Care of Fibreglass Poles', p.10.)

TRAINING FOR YOUNG VAULTERS

TECHNICAL TRAINING

The Approach (see Figs. 94-97 on p.61)
1. Run over laths — no pole.
2. Run over laths — with pole.
3. Run over low hurdles — no pole.
4. Run over low hurdles — with pole.

The Plant
1. Repeated plants on hurdle (Fig. 16).
2. Walk and plant.
3. Jog and plant.
4. Acceleration run and plant.
5. Short approach vault carrying the pole on the shoulder (Fig. 17) with the pole tip on the ground.

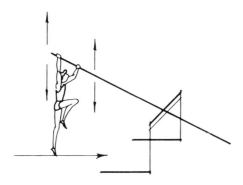

Fig. 16 Planting drills on a hurdle

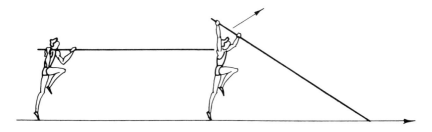

Fig. 17 Planting with the pole from a shoulder position

23

The Take-off

1. 4-6 stride vault into sand for distance.
2. 4-stride vault into landing area.
3. Vault into landing area with no box.

With this exercise it is important that the pole be placed in a vertical position before the athlete jumps so that the pole does not slip on the ground.

GYMNASTIC EXERCISES

Ropes

1. Rope climbs.
2. Repeated swings and turns.
3. Swing on rope over bar from box.
4. Run and swing on rope over bar.

Tumbling

1. Backward roll.
2. Backward roll to handstand (Fig. 18).
3. Handstands.
4. Walking on hands.

Fig. 18 Backward roll to handstand

STRENGTH

For young vaulters strength training should be confined to body-weight exercises arranged in the form of a circuit. Dorsal and abdominal training is the main priority and the concentration should be on good all-round physical development. Suitable exercises include:

Skipping
Wall Jumps (Fig. 19)
Squat Thrusts
Leg raises on the floor (Fig. 20)
Sit-ups with bent legs
Hyperextensions on the floor (Fig. 21)
Press-ups
Pillars
Pull-ups from inclined position (Fig. 22)

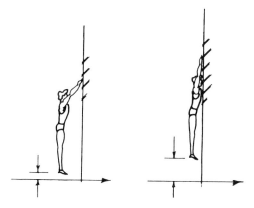

Fig. 19 Wall jumps

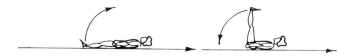

Fig. 20 Leg raises on the floor

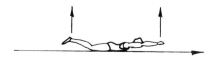

Fig. 21 Hyperextensions on the floor

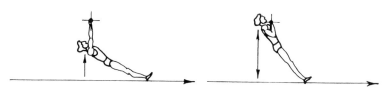

Fig. 22 Pull ups from inclined position

RUNNING

Running for young vaulters should be varied and should concentrate on developing a good running posture and good all-round endurance. Running will include some trackwork but during the winter months should involve cross-country running and similar activities.

It is important that young vaulters should be encouraged to participate in a wide variety of sports and activities. Participation in other athletic events and other sports will develop all-round fitness and skills which ultimately will be of enormous benefit to the vaulter.

GROUP ACTIVITIES (at clubs or schools)

OUTDOOR ACTIVITIES

Equipment Required

1. A selection of small metal, bamboo or fibreglass training poles.
2. A box.
3. A sand-pit.
4. An elastic bar.
5. Canes.

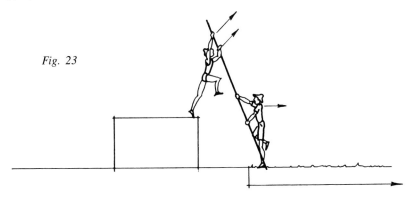

Fig. 23

(a) Vaulting into sand-pit from a box (Fig. 23).

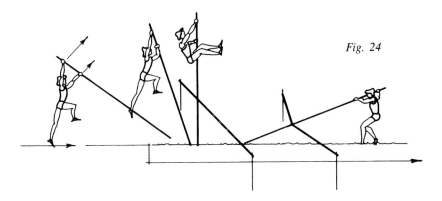

Fig. 24

(b) Vaulting into sand-pit over an elastic bar (Fig. 24).

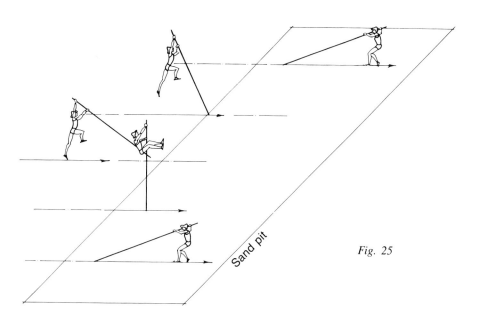

Fig. 25

(c) Swinging on pole into sand-pit (Fig. 25).

One or two stride approach. Plant the pole in the sand, take-off, swing, turn and land in the sand facing the opposite direction to the one the vaulter has come from.

Fig. 26

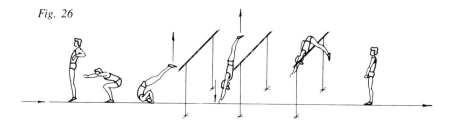

(d) Backward roll to handstand over an elastic bar (Fig. 26).

Outdoor Activity Circuit (Fig. 27)

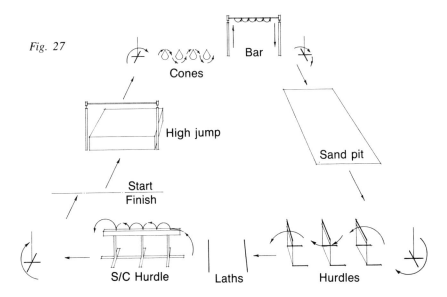

Fig. 27

Cones

Bar

High jump

Sand pit

Start
Finish

S/C Hurdle

Laths

Hurdles

INDOOR ACTIVITIES

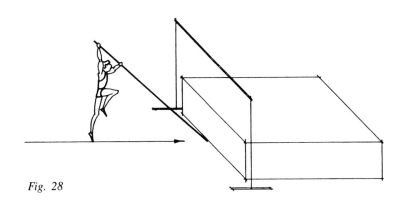

Fig. 28

(a) Short approach vault on to mat (Fig. 28).

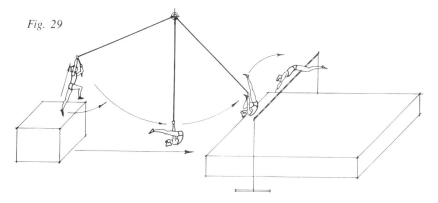

Fig. 29

(b) Rope vault from box over elastic (Fig. 29).

Fig. 30

(c) Drop upstart on beam (Fig. 30).

Indoor Activity Circuit (Fig. 31)

Fig. 31

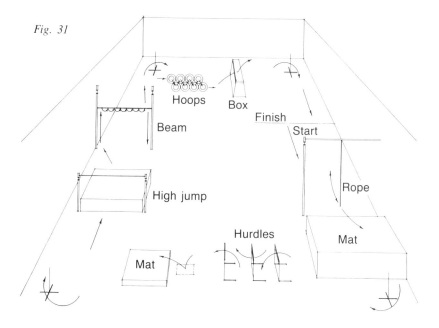

Hoops

Box

Finish

Start

Beam

High jump

Rope

Hurdles

Mat

Mat

CHECKLIST

	Technique	Drills	Physical Training

STAGE ONE
On ground
	Grip
	Handhold
	2-stride approach
	Left-foot take-off
	Swing right side of
	  pole
	Turn
	Land on feet
		Practise pole carry
		Practise plant on
		  hurdles
			Cross-country
			Multi-events
			Swings on ropes
			Games

STAGE TWO Into sand	Higher grip 4-6 stride approach Straight top arm Plant in sand Swing Lift legs Turn and land on feet		
STAGE THREE Landing area	Correct grip Higher grip 6-8 stride approach Correct plant action Use of elastic bar Legs higher	Runs over laths Plant drills Vaults into sand	Cross-country Multi-events Gymnastic exercises Body-weight strength exercises Flexibility Games

STAGE FOUR
Landing area
	10-stride approach
	Smooth acceleration
	Early plant
	Vigorous take-off
	Swing
	Turn
	Clearance
	Push-away pole
		Runs over laths
		Runs over low
		  hurdles
		Acceleration runs
		  with plant
		Plant drills
		Take-off drills
		Short approach
		  vaults
			Cross-country
			Multi-events
			Gymnastic exercises
			Body-weight
			  strength exercises
			Various sports
			Flexibility

STAGE FIVE
Bending the
  Pole
	Choose suitable pole
	6-8 stride approach
	Early, fast and high
	  plant
	Keep pole away
	  from the body
	Progress to extended
	  left leg swing		

POLE VAULTING TECHNIQUE

THE GRIP AND POLE CARRY

A correct grip and pole carry is essential if the vaulter is to be in a position to execute an efficient plant and take-off. The TOP HAND of the vaulter should hold the pole at the hip, palm facing forward with the pole resting between the thumb and the first finger. The arm should be bent at 90°. The BOTTOM HAND should grasp the pole palm downwards with the arm again bent at the elbow at 90° (see Fig. 32). Vaulters should be careful to avoid cocking the left wrist or allowing the right hand to move away from its position close to the hip.

Fig. 32 The grip and carry

Alternatively many vaulters prefer to close the right hand around the pole during the approach (see Fig. 33), but this often leads to the hand moving away from the hip and can cause problems with the plant. More recently some vaulters using very high grips hold the pole in front of the hips in order to keep a correct posture and facilitate an early plant (see Fig. 34). With such a grip the pole tip will be held high with the left hand held close to the chest. If such a carry is used it is essential that the pole is lowered gradually during the course of the approach and not at the moment when the plant action is initiated two strides from take-off. In what might be termed an orthodox grip the pole tip will be held at eye level or just above, pointing slightly to the left.

Fig. 33 Closed grip

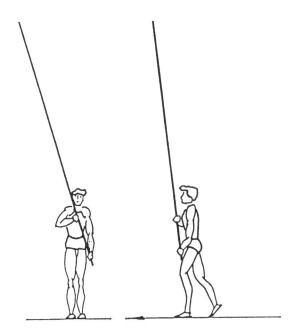

Fig. 34 The high carry

The hand-spread on the pole must be sufficiently wide to allow the vaulter to run with the pole and control it at take-off, but not too wide so as to impair the vaulter's ability to swing and rock back. In contrast to the early days of fibreglass vaulting, today's poles permit a much narrower handspread and certainly the hands should not be more than shoulder width apart. Providing that the vaulter can control his pole during the approach and at take-off, a narrow handspread (i.e. approximately 50-60 cms.) allows the vaulter to plant faster, to swing and rockback more easily and, most importantly, allows the lower left arm to work in conjunction with the top arm in driving the pole forward at and just after the take-off phase of the vault.

THE APPROACH
During the approach the vaulter attempts to generate the maximum controllable speed since ultimately the speed of the vaulter will determine the height he is able to achieve. The length of the run-up will depend upon the percentage of his top sprinting speed that he is capable of controlling at take-off and his ability to maintain a consistent stride pattern carrying a pole. In practice a vaulter will use a run-up of between 30 m. and 45 m.
    The key elements in a good approach are:

    (a) SPEED   (b) POSTURE   (c) STRIDE PATTERN

Speed
The best international vaulters reach speeds of 10 m/s, on the run-up, but control must not be sacrificed to speed. The vaulter must accelerate smoothly

32

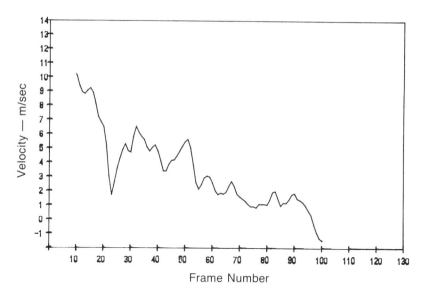

Fig. 35 Velocity loss profile of Earl Bell (U.S.A.) at take-off. (The Plant takes place at Frame 17)

and should avoid overstriding. In particular there should be no loss of speed over the last six strides and, although inevitably there will be some loss of speed at take-off, the ability to restrict this loss to a minimum is a key element in a successful vault. Undoubtedly the future development of the event lies in improving the efficiency of this phase of the vault.

Posture

A correct posture is essential if the vaulter wishes to take advantage of the speed he has generated and execute a vigorous and forceful take-off. The vaulter should maintain an upright posture. A slight forward lean is preferable to leaning backwards — a common fault with beginners, especially if the pole is heavy. A full extension of the driving leg is essential and "running tall" best describes the action of the vaulter during this stage. Pumping the arms during the run is not desirable and should be avoided — a relaxed yet determined attitude should be aimed at.

Fig. 36a Posture during approach

33

Fig. 36b Sergei Bubka (U.S.S.R.) — The Approach

Stride Pattern

As with all jumping events, a consistent stride pattern is critical if the vaulter is to take-off from the correct position. The approach run can be divided into three phases:

variable	8 - 16 strides	6 - 8 strides
(a)	(b)	(c)

The beginning of the run (a) will vary according to individual vaulters, some preferring to begin from a standing position, some by walking or jogging a few paces, and others with a few springy steps. The second phase (b) sees the vaulter begin to accelerate smoothly. The stride pattern takes shape and the vaulter adopts a good relaxed body position. The final phase (c) sees an increase in the stride rate and height of the knees with the vaulter approaching the take-off point in an aggressive and determined fashion. The last stride before take-off will usually be slightly shorter than the preceding strides (too long a last stride will lower the centre of gravity of the vaulter and adversely affect his take-off.

At take-off the vaulter's centre of gravity should be directly over the take-off foot (see Fig. 11 on p.20).

In order to assist the vaulter to take-off consistently from the correct position, it is often desirable to use checkmarks. Most commonly the vaulter will use a checkmark at the beginning of his run and sometimes also at a point 10-12 strides from take-off. In addition many coaches employ a checkmark 6 strides from take-off to judge the efficiency of the vaulter over the last strides before take-off.

THE PLANT

The purpose of the plant is to position the pole in the vaulting box in such a way as to enable the vaulter to take maximum advantage of the flexibility of the pole with the minimum loss of velocity. In fibreglass vaulting the plant must be *high, fast and early.* The plant action is initiated two strides from take-off. Although there have been many variations of pole plants, the most effective is that in which the pole is brought forwards and upwards. The action

34

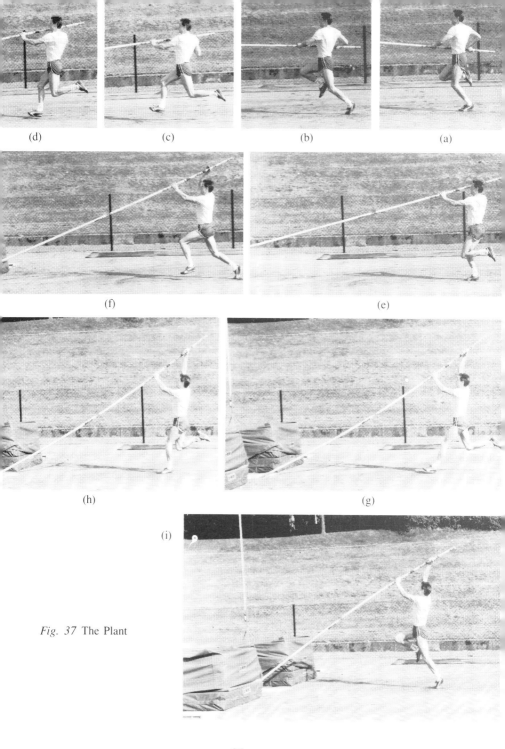

(d) (c) (b) (a)

(f) (e)

(h) (g)

(i)

Fig. 37 The Plant

35

of the top arm is similar to that of an uppercut in boxing and the arm should be kept close to the side of the body — a round arm action should be avoided.

The top arm should be fully extended above and slightly in front of the head at the moment the take-off foot touches the ground. The plant action must be completed fractionally before the bottom of the pole hits the back of the vaulting box.

At the completion of the plant:

(a) the vaulter should be square on to the box with the pole directly in front.

(b) the chest must lean into the pole and lead the body forward.

(c) the eyes should be looking between the hands, not down towards the box.

(d) the take-off leg should be fully extended with the vaulter as tall as possible.

The purpose of the lower arm during the plant should be to assist in bending and directing the pole and to keep the vaulter's body behind and away from the pole. To this end the lower arm should be kept rigid (whether bent at the elbow or not) with the elbow slightly to the side of the pole rather than directly in line with it, and should not collapse into the pole.

Fig. 38 Sergei Bubka (U.S.S.R.) — The Plant

36

THE TAKE-OFF AND SWING

The take-off in the pole vault is very similar to that in the long jump and should be executed with a vigorous driving action of the non take-off knee. The take-off foot should be positioned directly under a straight line drawn from the vaulter's raised upper hand to the ground. (Although many excellent performances are achieved by vaulters who take off either in front of or behind this position and who utilize their speed and strength more advantageously by altering the take-off position, height at take-off transcends all other factors and should determine the position of the take-off foot.) See Figs. 37 and 38.

Immediately after take-off the non take-off knee should continue to drive forward and upward and should not be dropped, even to aid penetration. The take-off leg should be pushed backwards and kept extended, both to aid penetration and to assist the vaulter's swing. The time the vaulter "hangs" in this position will depend upon a number of factors, the most important being the height of the vaulter's grip upon his pole and the stiffness of the pole.

During the hang and swing phase the action of the upper arm is most important, more especially so if the vaulter is using a high grip. The upper arm (assisted by the lower arm if the handspread is sufficiently narrow) should actively drive the pole forward into the box. The forward movement of the pole will enable the vaulter to proceed with a vigorous swing and rock back action without stalling out. It is important that during this phase the lower arm should be kept as rigid as possible and should not collapse into the pole.

Fig. 39 The Hang

The swing phase should be completed as fast as possible with the take-off leg remaining straight. Delaying the swing will increase the vaulter's penetration but will reduce his speed and impair his ability to reach an effective extended position on the pole. The rock back position will follow naturally on from the swing and should be achieved before or by the time the pole reaches its maximum bend. In the rock back position the vaulter will have his back parallel to the ground with his legs bent at the knees. Throwing the head back during this stage may assist the vaulter to achieve an early rock back, but is likely also to lead to the vaulter "stalling out".

If the correct rock back position is assumed, the vaulter will be in a position

37

to elevate his hips and legs and take maximum advantage of the recoil of the pole. There should be as little delay as possible in reaching a fully extended position and the support phase on the pole should be as short as possible. Excessive time spent on the pole during the support phase of the vault will have the effect of slowing down the vaulter and he will be unable to take advantage of the pole's recoil. Although excellent results have been achieved by vaulters assuming a closely tucked position in the pre-extension phase (e.g. Vigneron), it would seem that a continual and vigorous elevation of the legs and hips back to the pole (similar to the action of a gymnast on a high bar) is more efficient and will allow the vaulter to take full advantage of the recoil of the pole. The support time on the pole will also be lessened, thereby assuring that the speed of the pole's recoil is as fast as possible.

Fig. 40a Sergei Bubka (U.S.S.R.) — The Swing

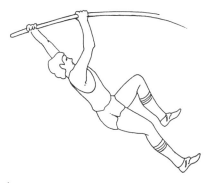

Fig. 40b The Swing

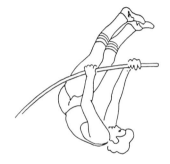

Fig. 40c The closely tucked position

Fig. 40d Vaulter covering the bend of the pole with his legs

THE EXTENSION

To gain maximum advantage from the extension the vaulter must adopt an active rather than passive role. The vaulter's body should be tensed and kept as straight as possible. The lower arm is responsible for keeping the body close to the pole and the upper arm, which remains straight, should pull directly down the line of the pole. The timing of the pull is critical and must coincide with the vaulter's hip elevation and the pole's recoil. The turn should be delayed for as long as possible but in practice will coincide with the extension.

Fig. 41 The Extension

BAR CLEARANCE

The vaulter's position over the bar is largely the result of his technique earlier in the vault. Both flyaway and jack-knife techniques are employed by international vaulters, but whichever style is preferred it is important that during the clearance the vaulter's centre of gravity should be kept above his handgrip. To assist this the vaulter should drop his legs by flexing at the hips. When the hips are clear of the bar, the vaulter should avoid throwing his arms backwards as this may cause his chest to dislodge the bar. He should depress his stomach and turn his hands inwards moving his elbows out of the way and preventing his arms from brushing the bar off.

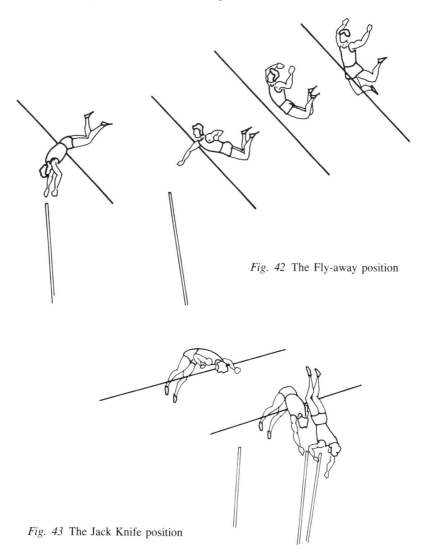

Fig. 42 The Fly-away position

Fig. 43 The Jack Knife position

TRAINING FOR THE POLE VAULT

To vault well, a vaulter requires not only a sound technique but also the physical qualities of a sprinter, jumper and gymnast. The vaulter's training will need to incorporate a wide variety of disciplines designed to improve his speed, strength, gymnastic ability and technique and his overall competitiveness.

PHYSICAL TRAINING

1. THE WARM-UP

A thorough warm-up is essential as preparation for all training sessions. It will help to prepare the body for the demands to be made upon it. It will also help avoid injuries and it will prepare the athlete mentally. Although every athlete will adopt a warm-up to suit his own personal needs, the temperature and the nature of the training session will vary; generally speaking a warm-up will last for 20 mins. to 30 mins. and will consist of the following:

(a) General warm-up
   1. Jogging
   2. Striding 80-100 m.
   3. Stretching

(b) Specific warm-up
   1. Short sprints with and without a pole
   2. Practice plants
   3. Practice vaults.

2. RUNNING

Pole vaulters are above all else runners and jumpers and the ability to harness their speed on the run-up will largely determine the success of their vaulting. The best vaulters are top class sprinters and much of the track work a vaulter will do is geared towards improving his speed and his ability to use that speed in a vault. The main element of a vaulter's running can be broken down into the following:

(a) Endurance training

(b) Speed work

(c) Running technique

Endurance Training

As with other athletic events, a vaulter needs to be fit to train if he is to cope with the intense demands of high level training and if he is to avoid injuries. Running represents the most effective means of achieving an overall level of fitness on which a vaulter can begin to build a comprehensive training programme. As part of their conditioning programme vaulters should make use of cross-country running (3-6 miles), slow constant running (2-6 miles), fartleks and interval training.

Examples of Endurance Training for Vaulters

Method	Frequency	Description
Interval Training	1-2 per week	2 × 600 m. 3 × 200 m. 70% max.
Slow Running	1 per week	4-6 kms. at slow steady pace (e.g. $7\frac{1}{2}$ minutes a km. pace)
Cross-country	1 per week	5000 m. training or races
Fartlek	1 per week	Jog 10 mins., run 2-3 kms. at fast steady pace, walk 7 mins., alternate jog/sprint (30 m.) for 2 mins., sprint uphill 100-150 m., jog 1-2 kms.

Speed

A vaulter must learn to approach the take-off box with the maximum controllable speed he can generate. His speed training must be directed to this end. In addition the vaulter needs to be able to repeat his approach many times and needs to be at his best towards the conclusion of the competition. Speed training therefore should be designed not only to improve a vaulter's speed but also to improve his ability to use that speed repeatedly.

Speed Endurance

This can be achieved by using the following methods:

(a) Repetition sprints — 40-150 m. e.g. 2 × 5 × 60 m., walkback recovery, 3 mins. between sets.

(b) Hollow sprints — Sprint 50 m., jog 50 m., walk 50 m. over distance of 600 m.

Speed Increase

This training should be done with as well as without poles since it is important for the vaulter to adapt his running technique at speed to the slightly different technique required for running with a pole.

(a) Repetition sprints — 30-60 m. e.g. Repeated maximum speed sprints with full recovery between sprints.

(b) Acceleration runs — 40-100 m. Gradual acceleration to maximum speed. Full recovery between repetitions.

(c) Sprint drills — High knees, fast feet.

Summary

Running will be a year round activity for vaulters. In general, endurance training will be confined to the conditioning phase of training in October and November, speed endurance will form part of a vaulter's preparation phase and speed work will form the basis of training during the technical or competition phase of a programme.

3. STRENGTH

Strength will be a key element in a vaulter's success. Improvements in strength are constantly required to improve the vaulter's speed, his ability to handle stiffer and longer poles and to perform the necessary gymnastic exercises on the pole. Equally important, strength will give the vaulter the confidence he needs if he is to vault really high.

The young vaulter's requirements are somewhat different to those of the more experienced vaulter. Initially the young vaulter will concentrate on body weight exercises with the emphasis being placed on strengthening the abdominal-dorsal region.

Body weight circuit exercises are ideal for this. As the athlete progresses he will move on to more general strength exercises, perhaps by the age of 15-16 years using a multi-gym or similar apparatus. Gradually more specific exercises will be introduced and eventually the vaulter will need to make use of free weights.

For senior vaulters, different types of strength will be required for the different elements of a vault and more specific training is needed. However it must always be remembered that to achieve efficient results and to avoid injuries several years of general strength training will be needed by every athlete.

The basic types of strength work required by vaulters are as follows:

(a) **Strength Endurance** — necessary as part of the conditioning of a vaulter, but also needed if the vaulter is to perform a large number of vaults at a high level. It is achieved by:

1. *Isotonic Exercises* — e.g. 3 × 20-30, 30-40% 1RM, 2-3 times per week.

   Suitable exercises for vaulters could include:

   $\frac{1}{2}$ squats
   Bench press
   Upright rowing
   Sit-ups
   Power cleans
   Hyperextensions
   Bent over rowing (narrow grip)
   Tricep bench press with dumbells
   High pull-up
   Military press
   Calf raises
   Hamstring curls

2. *Circuit Training* — e.g. 2-3 sets, 1-2 minutes per exercise, 2-3 times per week.

   Tuck jumps
   Sit-ups (bent legs; feet on or off the ground)
   Press-ups
   Squat thrusts
   Wall jumps
   Hyperextensions
   Chinnies

43

Basketball throws against the wall
V-sits
Shuttle runs

3. *Skipping* — a form of plyometric training which is much underrated. Extremely valuable for vaulters, not only as a form of conditioning but also to improve mobility, strength and coordination.

An example of a session for vaulters might be:

2 × 2-3 minutes of skipping, varying the pace every 20-30 secs.

(b) **Maximum Strength** — essential to improve speed and the vaulter's ability to control his pole at and immediately after take-off. Strength programmes must concentrate on the following muscle groups: the gluteus maximus, the quadriceps femoris, the gastroenemius, the iliopsoas, the dorsal and ventral muscles, the triceps brachii and the pectoralis major.

Suitable exercises for vaulters could include:

Half squats
Power cleans
Snatch
Calf raises
Leg curls
Press behind neck
Bench press
Straight arm pullover
Hyperextensions
Sit-ups

As part of a vaulter's strength programme six to eight exercises should be selected. Training should be three times per week with each session including 5-7 sets of 2-8 repetitions at 70-95% of 1 RM. Exercising speed should be slow to explosive.

(c) **Specific Strength** — necessary for the athlete to perform certain manoeuvres specific to vaulting.

Specific strength can be acquired primarily through gymnastics (see gymnastics section) and by incorporating certain exercises into a weekly or twice weekly circuit. Suitable exercises would include work using ropes and wall bars and floor work with vaulting poles.

1. *Ropes*

Speed climbs up rope (no feet)
Speed climbs up rope upside down
Swing to rock-back and extension on rope (Fig. 44)
Swing on rope from box over a bar (Fig. 45)
Run and swing on rope over a bar (Fig. 46)

2. *Wall bars*

Leg raises on wall bars
Leg raises on wall bars holding at three positions (Fig. 47)
Lateral leg raises on wall bars to extension position (Fig. 48)

3. *Floor exercises with pole vault pole*

Sit-ups with a pole (Fig. 49)

Rock-back and extension up pole (Fig. 50)
Rock-back and extension through pole (Fig. 51)
Hyperextensions with a pole (Fig. 52)

Fig. 44 Swing to rock, rock back and extension on rope

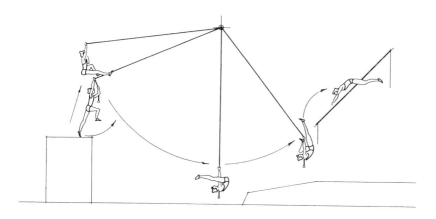

Fig. 45 Swing on rope from box over an elastic bar

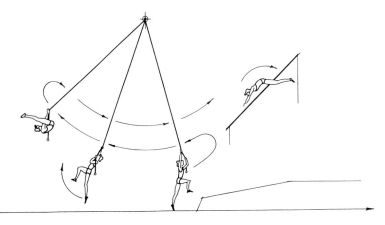

Fig. 46 Run and swing on rope over an elastic bar

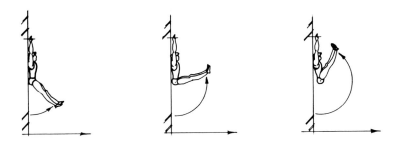

Fig. 47 Leg raises on wall bars, holding at three positions

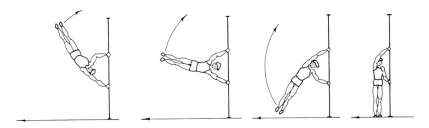

Fig. 48 Lateral leg raises on wall bars to extension position

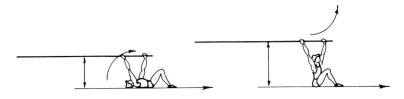

Fig. 49 Sit-ups with a pole

46

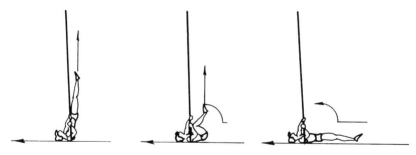

Fig. 50 Rock-back and extension up a pole

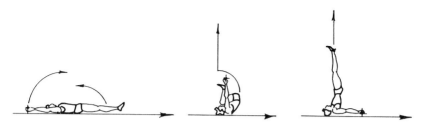

Fig. 51 Rock-back and extension through pole

Fig. 52 Hyperextension with a pole

(d) **Elastic Strength** — Essential for the development of the explosive strength necessary for the improvement of a vaulter's jumping ability. As such it represents one of the most critical areas of vault training, all the more so since it is an area of training which has seen some major advances in methodology in recent years. Training revolves round the use of plyometric exercises which can put severe strains on athletes and is therefore to be used only by experienced athletes who are fully fit, well-conditioned and conversant with the correct techniques. Young athletes can be introduced to simple plyometric exercises such as skipping and hopping but should refrain from the more strenuous exercises such as bounding and depth jumping.

If used properly the benefits of plyometric training are enormous since it is primarily related to that crucial area of the vault, the take-off. Improvement in the jumping ability of a vaulter can produce startling effects on the height achieved and much of the recent improvements in vaulting have come about as a result of the increased jumping ability of present day vaulters.

For vaulters plyometric training should consist of the following:

1. *For conditioning* — hop 30 m. on right leg and bound back 30 m. to start; then hop 30 m. on left leg and bound back 30 m. to start; then double leg jump to 30 m. and sprint back to start. Repeat 2-3 times. 3-5 mins. of active rest between repetitions.

2. *For endurance:* — skipping — 2-3 minutes
   — bounding — 2 sets of 4 × 80-100 m.
   1 minute rest between repetitions,
   5 minutes between sets
   — box work — variety of hops and bounds over and on to 3-4 boxes over 60 m.

3. *For power* — Bounding — 3 sets of 5 repetitions bounding for distance over 60 m.
   1 minute rest between repetitions,
   5 minutes between sets
   — Depth jumping — 10 jumps (height determined by ability of athletes)
   — Depth jumps with rebound.

Upper body plyometric exercises can also be of value. Particularly useful are exercises involving the use of medicine balls and basketballs.

e.g. Overhead medicine ball throws from standing position.

Overhead medicine ball throw from sitting position (feet on or off the ground).

Medicine ball throws from the chest from sitting position (feet on or off ground).

Fast rebound throws with a basketball against the wall (overhead and from chest).

ADVANCED STRENGTH TRAINING FOR POLE VAULTERS

For advanced performers, probably the most efficacious form of training for the development of explosive strength is the Soviet inspired complex training. This consists of a blend of exercises using heavy or near maximum loads followed by exercises involving fast muscle responses. The concept uses the principle that muscle responses will be much faster after the use of heavy loadings than would normally be the case.

This form of training is extremely beneficial for the development of jumping strength and also has the advantage of being versatile and interesting. The main disadvantages are the amount of time required to complete a complex and the additional facilities which may be needed.

Possible complexes for vaulters might be as follows:

(a) $\frac{1}{2}$ squats: 2 × 2-3 repetitions at 90% of 1RM.
3 minutes between sets (stretching). 6 minutes after both sets.
Bounding: 40-50 m. at full speed. 4 repetitions.
3 minutes between repetitions. 6 minutes after all repetitions.
Acceleration runs: 75 m. gradually increasing speed.
15 minutes recovery — jogging and mobility work — then repeat complex.

(b) Calf raises: 2 × 2-3 repetitions at 90% of 1RM.
3 minutes between sets (stretching). 6 minutes after both sets.
Jumps over hurdles: 2 × 5 over 4 hurdles.
3 minutes between repetitions. 6 minutes after both sets.
15 minutes recovery — jogging and mobility work. Repeat calf raises.
Short sprints: 5 × 50 m. 30 seconds between repetitions.

(c) Upper body complex.
Bench press: 2 × 3 repetitions at 90% 1RM.
3 minutes between sets (stretching). 6 minutes after both sets.
Medicine ball throws: 2 × 10.
3 minutes between sets.
15 minutes recovery after complex (jogging and stretching).
Repeat bench press.
Basketball rebounds against wall 2 × 45 seconds.
3 minutes between sets.

Complex training makes heavy demands upon an athlete's body. It should not be attempted by inexperienced athletes or by athletes who have not had several years of sound conditioning work.

4. GYMNASTICS

The highly complex manoeuvres that skilled vaulters need to perform on the pole make it imperative that gymnastics play an important role in the training of a vaulter. Gymnastic strength, agility, spacial awareness, body tension and the similarity of many of the movements performed by gymnasts and vaulters all combine to make gymnastics a vital part of a vaulter's training.

Gymnastics should be an all year round activity undertaken at least once a week. Exercises should be progressive related to a vaulter's age, strength and experience. Preferably a gymnastics coach should be prevailed upon to ensure correct techniques are used.

Exercises most valuable to the vaulter include the following:

(a) *Floor Exercises*

Forward rolls
Backward rolls
Backward rolls to handstand
Crouch jump
Handstand
Handspring
Flik-flak
Forward somersault
Backward somersault
Walking on hands

(b) *Rings*

Rock-back and extension
Skin the cat
Handstands

(c) *Beam*

Upward circle
Heave vault

(d) *High Bar*

Muscle ups
Upstart
Upward circle
Swing to handstand

(e) *Parallel Bars*

Swing to handstand
From hanging position, rock-back and extension

(f) *Body Tension Exercises*

Fixed dish exercises — Figs. 53-55

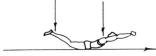

Fig. 53 Static arch   *Fig. 54* Static 'dish' shape on front

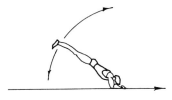

Fig. 55 Dish shaped body raising and lowering

(g) *Strand Exercises*

See Figs. 56-59

Fig. 56

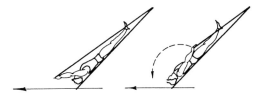

Fig. 57

50

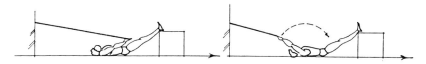

Fig. 58

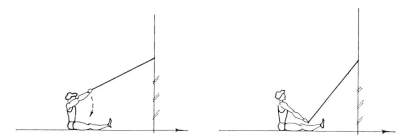

Fig. 59

5. MOBILITY

Even a perfect vault places tremendous strain on the vaulter's body, and even the best vaulters have bad vaults. Taking off too far away from the box or too close will subject the vaulter to pressures he must be fit enough to combat. Flexibility training in conjunction with his strength work can minimise the risk of injury and must form a regular part of a vaulter's programme.

Frequency and Duration

Stretching sessions should be performed between 5 and 7 days a week throughout the year, with each session lasting approximately 30 minutes. A sample programme of active and passive stretching exercises suitable for a vaulter is as follows:

1. *Shoulders and Neck*
   (a) Stand with arms outstretched in front, feet slightly apart. Circle arms slowly downwards, backwards and over the head. 20 repetitions, then reverse direction.

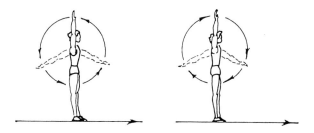

Fig. 60

(b) Stand upright with the feet slightly apart, arms by the side. Drop the shoulders. Move right ear towards right shoulder. Hold for 20 secs. then repeat with the left ear.

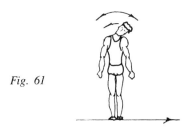

Fig. 61

2. *Wrist*

Place the palms of the hands flat on the floor with the fingers facing away from the body. Keeping the elbows straight and the palms flat on the floor, rotate the hands outwards and bring the fingers to face the body. Hold for 30 secs.

Fig. 62

3. *Back/Hips*

(a) Sit on the floor with the legs as far apart as possible, hands stretched in front touching the floor. Move hands forward away from the body as far as possible. Hold for 1 min.

Fig. 63

Plan

(b) Crab Position. Lie on back on the floor. Bring the feet as close to the buttocks as possible, while keeping them flat on the floor. Raise the hands over the shoulders to touch the ground with the fingers as close as possible to the shoulders, palms flat on the ground, fingers pointing inwards. Raise the hips as high as possible, straightening the arms and legs. Hold for 20 secs.

Fig. 64

(c) Sit on the floor, legs wide apart, hands behind the head. Turn right elbow down to and past the left knee, keeping the legs flat on the floor. Hold for 30 secs. and repeat with the left elbow.

(d) Stand with the feet together, arms by the sides. Step well forward with the right foot and at the same time swing right arm upwards and backwards as far as possible. Hold for 1 min.

Fig. 65

(e) Stand with the back to the wall. Keeping the feet stationary, turn to the right and place the palms of the hands on the wall. Hold for 30 secs. then repeat on the other side.

(f) Lie on back on the the floor, feet together and outstretched, arms perpendicular to the body. Keeping the legs straight, raise the left leg and touch the right hand with the left foot. Hold for 15 secs. and repeat with the right leg.

(g) Lie on back and raise the feet straight into the air, supporting the hips with the hands. Point the toes and touch the right foot to the floor above the head. Hold for 15 secs. and repeat with the other foot.

Fig. 66

4. *Ankle*

Standing upright, rise high on to the right toe, keeping the left foot on the floor. Lower right foot and raise left foot, keeping the right foot flat on the floor. 20 repetitions.

5. *Legs*

(a) Lie flat on the back on the floor with legs outstretched in front, feet together. Raise the right foot in the air and slowly move the foot towards the head, keeping the leg straight. If necessary use a partner

Fig. 67

53

or a belt round the foot to ease the leg back as far as possible. Hold for 1 min. and repeat with the left leg.

(b) Stand several feet in front of a wall with the feet slightly apart. Place the outstretched hands on the wall, keeping the feet flat on the floor. Slowly move them away from the wall, still keeping them flat on the floor. Hold for 1 min.

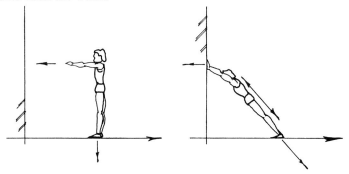

Fig. 68

(c) Sit on the floor with the legs apart. Keeping the legs straight, reach for the right foot, grasp and hold for 30 secs. Repeat with the left foot.

(d) Sit on the floor with the soles of the feet touching each other in front. Slowly push down on the knees as far as possible with the hands or elbows. Hold for 30 secs.

(e) Sit on the heels, knees together. Allow the buttocks to settle on the floor, keeping the toes turned inwards and heels outwards. Gradually lean backwards until resting on the elbows. Hold for 1 min.

A more effective but slightly more time-consuming way of stretching is the Proprioceptive Neuromuscular Facilitating (P.N.F.) method. This will involve stretching the muscle as far as possible by the passive method of stretching, then contracting the muscle, relaxing, followed by stretching the muscle (a little further this time), contracting the muscle again and relaxing. The entire routine should then be repeated. For most exercises a partner will be required and care should be taken that muscles are not over-stretched.

The following exercises are suitable for vaulters using this method of stretching:

1. *Shoulders and Chest*

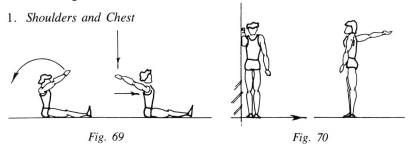

Fig. 69   *Fig. 70*

2. Calf Muscles

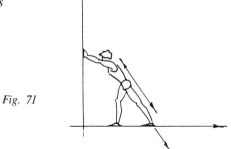

Fig. 71

3. Groin

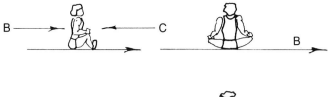

Fig. 72

4. Back

Fig. 73

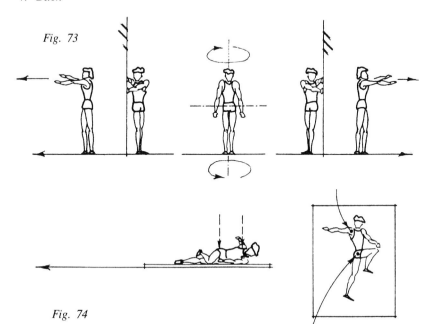

Fig. 74

5. *Quadriceps*

Fig. 75

6. *Iliopsoas*

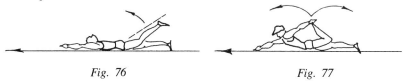

Fig. 76   *Fig. 77*

7. *Hamstrings*

Fig. 78   *Fig. 79*

Flexibility Parameters for Vaulters
1. *Knee Extension*

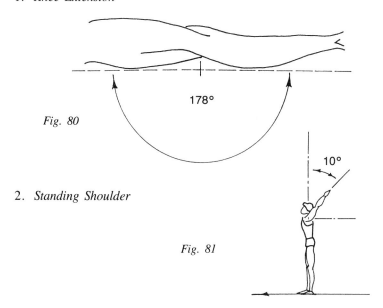

178°

Fig. 80

2. *Standing Shoulder*

10°

Fig. 81

3. *Handstand Shoulder flexibility*

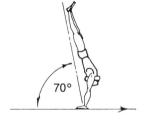

Fig. 82

70°

4. *Bridge Test (with straight legs and spine)*

Fig. 83

5. *Back Hang Shoulder*

Fig. 84

140°

6. *Straddled Legs body fold*

Fig. 85

15°

7. *Hamstring Test*

Fig. 86

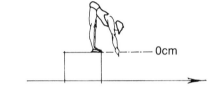

0cm

8. *Quadriceps and Hips*

Fig. 87

9. *Leg Hold (forwards)*

Fig. 88

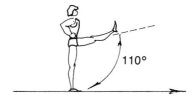

10. *Leg Hold (backwards)*

Fig. 89

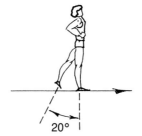

MENTAL TRAINING

Mental training is possibly the most neglected and undervalued component of an athlete's training — yet pole vaulting is very much an event which places great psychological strain on the athlete. Pole vaulting represents a challenge, and the greater the height attempted the greater the psychological barrier. To achieve world class performances a vaulter must be prepared to meet and overcome the psychological barriers which confront him.

The Role of the Coach

The role of the coach will be determined largely by his assessment of the athlete. It will depend upon the athlete's character and personality, his attitude to training and his disposition during competition. The coach will need to adopt a policy of positive or negative reinforcement towards the athlete which will vary depending upon particular circumstances and the mood of the athlete. The coach must take on the role of a teacher, moulding the character of his athlete, setting ambitious yet realistic goals and above all teaching the athlete the value of self-reliance.

The Successful Vaulter

The successful vaulter will be characterized by a total commitment to his event. He will be self-confident with the certain conviction that he can achieve his goals. He will have the ability to concentrate his mind on the task ahead and at the critical moment he will be able to utilize to the full all his physical and mental powers.

Training Techniques

(a) **Total Concentration** — the ability to focus attention on a single objective.

Methods
1. Sit quietly and become absorbed in a single object e.g. a tree, or a colour e.g. blue.
2. Use cue words such as 'early plant'.
3. Controlled slow, deep breathing.
4. Visualisation of perfect vaults or a particular aspect of a vault.

(b) **Emotional Control**

Methods
1. Use of relaxation techniques such as autogenic training and relaxation exercises.*
2. Positive dreaming — recall of good performances.

(c) **Peak Performance** — will require
1. Total immersion in the vault.
2. A feeling of complete control.
3. A positive attitude.
4. Motivation.
5. A feeling of power and an absence of strain.

Competition Planning

Immediately prior to an important competition the athlete should establish a routine suitable for his own particular needs. A typical routine might be:

2 days before competition : training session — fairly heavy

1 day before competition : wind down, totally different activity e.g. cinema etc.

Day of competition : Think positively about yourself. Think of your strengths.

The competition : Regular routine prior to warm-up. Total concentration.

Wind down Different activities	Sleep Relax Dream	Positive thinking Visualization	Total concentration Absorbtion in event Feeling of superiority
DAY	NIGHT		
1 Day Before		Day of Competition	Competition

---

* For further information and examples of exercises see B.A.A.B. Senior Coach Award Theory Manual and J. Syer and C. Connolly's 'Sporting Body Sporting Mind', pub. Simon and Schuster, 1987.

TECHNICAL TRAINING

A vaulter's technical training, like his physical training, will vary considerably depending upon the age and experience of the vaulter. It will consist not only of vaulting sessions using full or shortened approaches with high and low grips, but also the repetition of certain drills designed to simulate particular aspects of a vault and which in time will produce automatic muscle responses in the vaulter.

A. Drills and Exercises

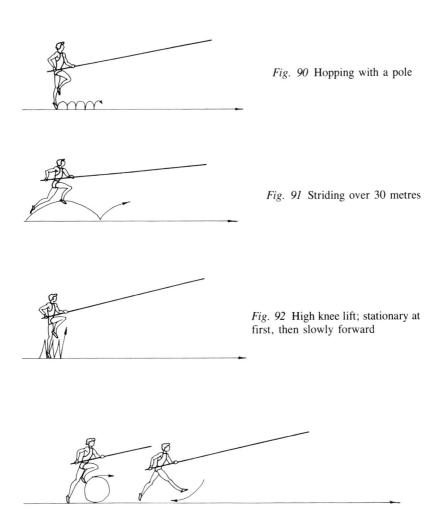

Fig. 90 Hopping with a pole

Fig. 91 Striding over 30 metres

Fig. 92 High knee lift; stationary at first, then slowly forward

Fig. 93 Trotting like a horse over 30 metres

Fig. 94 Gradually accelerating run with and without a pole over 30-40m

Fig. 95 Running with and without a pole over canes approximately 60cm apart

Fig. 96 Running with and without a pole over canes approximately 120-150cm apart

Fig. 97 Running with and without a pole over low hurdles

Fig. 98 Hopping over low hurdles with a pole

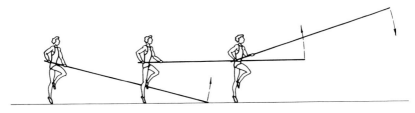

Fig. 99 Slow jogging with the pole being raised and lowered

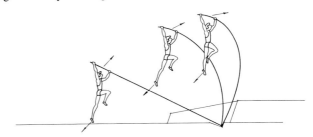

Fig. 100 For penetration — keep the legs hanging over the take-off

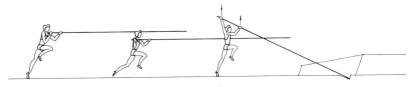

Fig. 101 Running with the pole on the shoulder, planting and take-off

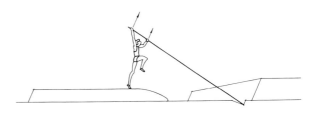

Fig. 102 Take-off from a raised platform or springboard

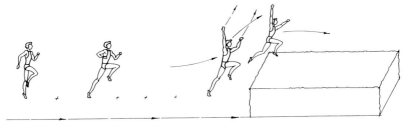

Fig. 103 Running from 5-7 strides and diving on to a box

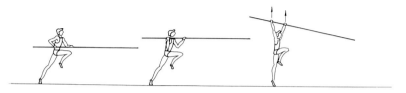

Fig. 104 Running over 30m raising and lowering the pole

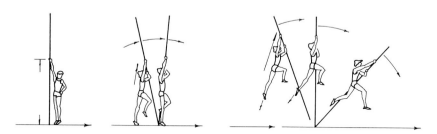

Fig. 105 Swinging on the pole, keeping the top arm straight and the left leg trailing as long as possible

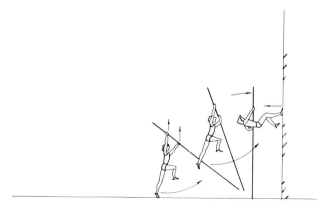

Fig. 106 Using the pole to swing the feet on to a wall

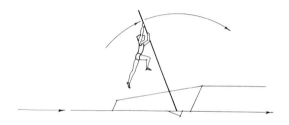

Fig. 107 Insert block into box. Vault without using a box

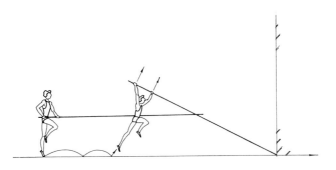

Fig. 108 Two stride approach and take-off

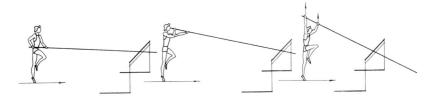

Fig. 109 Repeated plant action on a hurdle

Tyre

Fig. 110 Resistance running

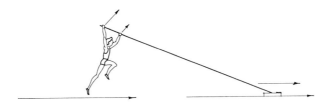

Fig. 111 Planting into a movable box

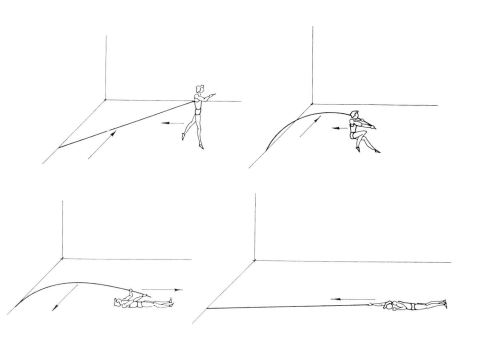

Fig. 112 Start from a standing position, bend the pole, lower the body to the floor and push off from the pole

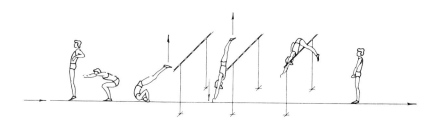

Fig. 113 Backward roll to handstand and push off over a bar

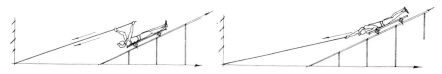

Fig. 114 Turn and push off on a movable trolley

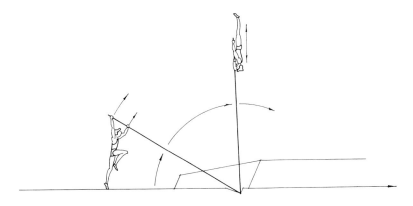

Fig. 115 A 'pop-up'

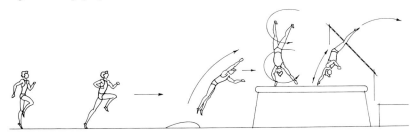

Fig. 116 Vaulting box exercise: 5 to 7 stride approach. The beginning of the jump is similar to a handspring or cartwheel. After take-off the vaulter swings into a momentary handstand. While the right hand acts as a support, the left hand pushes off. The vaulter then attempts to clear the bar in an arch-flyaway position

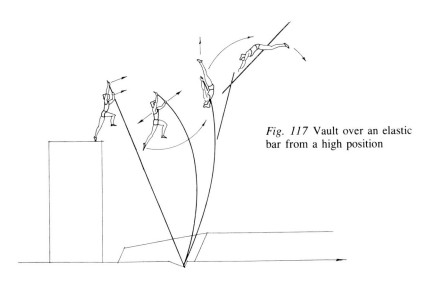

Fig. 117 Vault over an elastic bar from a high position

66

B. Vaulting

Vaulting will naturally form an essential part of a vaulter's training and he should learn to adapt to poles of varying lengths and flexes in a variety of different situations.

Vaulting sessions will include:

1. *Short Approach Vaults* — 4-6 strides using short training poles to work on plant and take-off.

2. *Medium Approach Vaults* — 10-12 strides, either using a handhold lower than that used in competition or a smaller pole, to work on a variety of different phases of the vault, or high grips to practise penetration techniques.

3. *Full Approach Vaults* — vaulting at heights above the vaulter's personal best.

Whatever pole is being used, vaulting sessions must never be haphazard. A session should be carefully regulated and the improvement of a specific aspect of technique must be the objective.

PLANNING YOUR TRAINING

The pole vault is an event which is demanding technically, physically and mentally and in consequence the athlete who wishes to perform at the highest levels requires a solid foundation of training. The preparation of a pole vaulter takes many years and should be accomplished in stages taking into account the individual characteristics and needs of each athlete. Training will be progressive with the emphasis being on skill acquisition in the formative years and moving towards a greater emphasis on physical development as the athlete matures. Development might be on the lines indicated in Figs. 118 and 119.

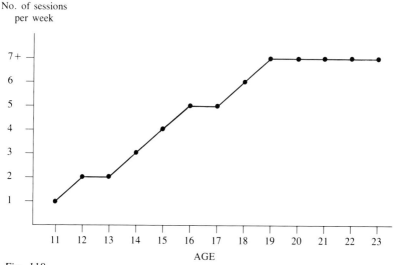

Fig. 118

67

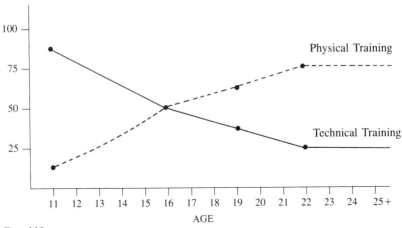

Fig. 119

ATHLETICS COACH

The Coaching Journal of the B.A.A.B.

Published:
March, June, September, December

Details from:
B.A.A.B. Coaching Office,
Edgbaston House,
3 Duchess Place,
Birmingham B16 8NM

The planning of training should be designed to gain maximum benefit from the work done by the athlete. Fig. 120 illustrates the extent to which age will affect the amount and type of training done by a vaulter.

The training year itself will be divided into periods called units, microcycles and macrocycles which taken together will constitute either a single or double periodized year.

Age	Sessions (per week)	Training	
		Physical	Technical
12 - 14	1 - 3	Cross-country Gymnastics Multi-events Various Sports Skipping Dorsal & Abdominal Exercises	Vaulting Pole Carry Drills Plant Drills Approach Drills
15 - 16	3 - 4	Endurance Running Sprinting Gymnastics Body Weight Circuit Exercises Various Sports Multi-events	Vaulting Plant Drills Approach Drills Rock-back & Extension Drills
17 - 20	4 - 7	Endurance Running Sprinting Gymnastics Weight Training Plyometrics Multi-events Specific Strength Exercises	Vaulting Drills
20 +	7 +	Endurance Running Sprinting Gymnastics Weight Training Plyometrics Specific Strength Exercises	Vaulting Drills

Fig. 120

TRAINING UNITS

Training units may be single or multiple and will generally last for $2-2\frac{1}{2}$ hours. Typical sessions might be as follows:

Single Training Unit

Warm-up   —   30-45 mins.

Vaulting Session	—	10-15 vaults with specific technical objective
		45-60 mins.
Warm-down	—	10-15 mins.

Multiple Training Unit

Warm-up	—	30-45 mins.
Vaulting Session	—	10-15 vaults with specific technical objective
		30-45 mins.
Warm-up	—	10-15 mins.
Vaulting Drills	—	30 mins.
Warm-down	—	10-15 mins.

Training units are combined into microcycles which may last for 7 to 21 days. Microcycles can be combined into mesocycles which in turn make up macrocycles. (For a more detailed explanation see B.A.A.B. Instructional Book 'Training Theory' by Frank Dick.)

An example of a one week microcycle for a vaulter:

Monday	:	Strength work		
Tuesday	:	Mobility	Track	
Wednesday	:	Vaulting	Drills	Dorsal & Abdominal Circuit
Thursday	:	Strength work		
Friday	:	Rest		
Saturday	:	Mobility	Gymnastics	
Sunday	:	Vaulting	Running Drills	Circuit Exercises

THE YEAR PLAN

Normally a year plan will take the form of a single periodized year when an athlete is preparing for a single competition period (usually the summer) or a double periodised year when the athlete wishes to compete both indoors and outdoors.

Single Periodised Year

Preparation						Competition				Transition	
Nov	Dec	Jan	Feb	Mar	Apr	May	June	July	Aug	Sept	Oct

Double Periodised Year

Preparation			Competition	Preparation		Competition				Transition	
Nov	Dec	Jan	Feb	Mar	Apr	May	June	July	Aug	Sept	Oct

Fig. 121 illustrates how a vaulter's training might be fitted into these training patterns.

70

	Oct	Nov	Dec	Jan	Feb	Mar	Apr	May	Jun	Jul	Aug	Sep
SINGLE PERIODISED YEAR												
Endurance		X										
Speed — Endurance		X	X	X	X	X	X	X	X	X	X	
General			X	X	X	X	X	X	X	X	X	
Specific		X	X	X	X	X	X					
Drills		X	X	X	X	X	X	X				
Gymnastics		X	X	X	X	X	X	X	X	X	X	X
Strength — General		X	X	X	X	X	X	X	X	X	X	X
Elastic		X	X	X	X	X	X	X				
Specific		X	X	X	X	X	X	X				
Mobility		X	X	X	X	X	X	X	X	X	X	X
Training Jumps		X	X	X	X	X	X	X				
Simulated Competition Jumps							X	X	X	X	X	X
Other Activities	X	X	X	X	X	X	X					
DOUBLE PERIODISED YEAR												
Endurance		X										
Speed — Endurance		X	X	X	X	X	X	X	X	X	X	
General			X	X	X	X	X	X	X	X	X	
Specific		X	X			X	X					
Drills		X	X			X	X					
Gymnastics		X	X	X	X	X	X	X	X	X	X	X
Strength — General		X	X	X	X	X	X	X	X	X	X	X
Elastic		X	X			X	X	X				
Specific		X	X			X	X	X				
Mobility		X	X	X	X	X	X	X	X	X	X	X
Training Jumps		X	X			X	X					
Simulated Competition Jumps				X	X	X		X	X	X	X	X
Other Activities	X	X	X			X	X					

Fig. 121

Endurance : Cross-country running. Interval training. Fartlek.

Speed — Endurance : Interval sprinting. Repetition running.

General : Repeated sprints at maximum speed with full recovery.

Specific : Acceleration sprints with pole.

71

Drills	: Exercises for various phases of the vault — carry, approach, plant, take-off, swing, extension, turn and clearance.
Gymnastics	: Exercises related to vaulting — especially use of high bar, wall bars, parallel bars, rope and vaulting box.
Strength — General	: Training with free weights.
Specific	: Exercises specific to vaulting using rope, wall-bars, high bar, etc.
Elastic	: Plyometrics.
Mobility	: Flexibility exercises in addition to those which form part of a warm-up and warm-down.
Training Jumps	: Short pole/soft pole/low grip — technique work using elastic bar.
Simulated Competition Jumps	: Higher grip, bigger poles, competition conditions.
Other Activities	: Long jumping and hurdles. Basketball and other games.

AN ALTERNATIVE YEAR PLAN FOR VAULTERS

Traditional year plans can cause problems for vaulters who find that the physical demands of their training impinge upon the technical work of vaulting. A vaulter needs to be fresh to vault effectively and even in training vaulters often need to use big poles and vault at heights above their personal bests.

To make the most of their strength work and their technical work a more complete separation of technical training and heavily loaded physical training is sometimes desirable.

The pattern for such a programme is shown below in Fig. 122.

Fig. 122

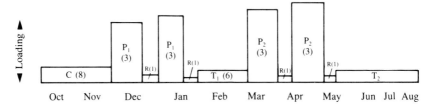

C : Conditioning Period — 8 weeks.
P1 : 2 × 4 week cycles consisting of 3 weeks highly loaded training followed by 1 week active rest, followed by 3 weeks loading (5-8% higher loading), followed by 1 week of active rest.
T1 : Technical Period — 6 weeks — technique work or competition.
P2 : Further 2 × 4 week cycles with approximately 5-8% higher loading than in P1.
T2 : Technical Period — competitive season — maximum 12 weeks.

72

The advantages of this system are that:

(a) Periods of low loading training produce maximum benefit from the strength training.

(b) Higher quality technical work is achieved by separating the technical and preparation periods.

(c) The system has great flexibility within the following guidelines:

1. Conditioning period should be no shorter than 4 and no longer than 12 weeks.

2. Preparation periods should be in blocks of 2-3 weeks.

3. Technical or competition periods should be no longer than 12 weeks.

4. For younger athletes the differential in loading between the preparation periods and technical periods will be limited and the beneficial effects of the system will be less.

Further examples can be seen in the Appendices.

TACTICS AND COMPETITION

THE RULES
Ensure that vaulters know the rules thoroughly. In particular certain aspects of the rules can cause confusion.

(a) The time that a vaulter is allowed for completing a vault may differ according to different circumstances.

(b) Provided a vaulter does not touch the ground or the landing area beyond the vertical plane of the upper part of the box with his pole or his body the fact that he may take off does *not* constitute a vault unless he dislodges the bar.

(c) It is a fallacy to suppose that if a competitor gets off the landing area after a vault before the bar is dislodged then it will not count as a failure.

WEATHER CONDITIONS
Wet Conditions
(a) Keep the pole grips dry. When checking the position of the uprights with a pole, use a pole you are not vaulting on if possible.

(b) If necessary use a smaller or softer pole.

(c) Use an adhesive substance on the pole.

(d) Change the pole grips regularly.

(e) Take an umbrella, plenty of towels and additional clothing to the competition.

Hot Conditions
(a) Keep out of the sun — use an umbrella or sunshade.

(b) Have plenty of water available to drink during the competition.

Cold Conditions
(a) Take plenty of clothing to the competition.

(b) Keep the hands warm.

(c) Warm-up thoroughly before and during the competition.

(d) Have warm drinks available.

THE POSITION OF THE STANDS
The position of the stands will vary according to the technique of the vaulter, the stiffness of the pole being used, the height being attempted, the depth of the box and the weather conditions.

As a general rule the better the vaulting conditions, e.g. a tailwind and a fast approach, the deeper the stands. The more adverse the conditions, e.g. a headwind, a shallow box and a slow approach, the closer the stands. A vaulter using a softer pole than usual will have his stands further back, while a vaulter using a stiffer pole than usual will vault with the stands further forward.

A vaulter should determine in training what is suitable for him and for his poles. However although the rules may permit it, for safety reasons vaulters should not vault with the stands situated in front of the vertical plane of the upper part of the box.

COMPETITION

The Warm-up

Vaulters must accustom themselves to situations where long intervals of time elapse between the time allotted for warm-up and the time when they are required to jump. In a long competition a vaulter may well need to warm-up more than once.

Poles

Many vaulters will use a variety of different poles during a competition depending upon the height, the weather conditions and the nature of the competition. In general, as a competition progresses a vaulter's grip may well go higher and he may use a stiffer pole. In qualifying competitions or in decathlon events a vaulter may well want to use a pole with which he knows he can safely clear a certain height.

Practice Vaults prior to a Competition

In major competitions these may be limited. Vaulters should ensure that they are versatile enough to cope with any restrictions that may be placed upon them.

Entry Heights

A vaulter should enter a competition at a height he can clear easily but not so low that he would be too tired later to vault effectively at the higher heights. During a competition it may well be worth while to miss out certain heights or, having failed at one height, to take one's remaining attempts at a higher height. Pay attention to your opponents' vaults.

BIBLIOGRAPHY AND RECOMMENDED READING

A.A.A. Handbook, current edition.

Athletics 1987, 1988, 1989, I.A.A.F.

Athletic Ability and the Anatomy of Motion, R. Wirfed-Wolfe Medical, 1984.

Athletes in Action, Ed. H. Payne, Pelham, 1985.

B.A.A.B. Senior Coaching Award Coaching Theory Manual, B.A.A.B.

Biomechanical Analysis of the Pole Vault, P.B. Sutcliffe, Athletics Coach, 1989.

British Athletics (Annual), B.A.A.B./N.U.T.S.

Encyclopaedia of Track and Field Athletics (5th Ed.), Ed. M. Watman, Robert Hale Ltd.

Guinness Book of Olympic Facts and Feats, S. Greenberg, Guinness Pubs.

I.A.A.F. Handbook, 1990/91.

In Pursuit of Excellence, T. Orlick, Human Kinetics Pub. Inc., 1975.

Mechanics of Athletics, G. Dyson, 8th Ed., Hodder & Stoughton, 1986.

Mechanics of the Pole Vault, D.V. Ganslen, 8th & 9th Eds., 1973, 1980.

Mental Training for Peak Performance, E. Gauron, Sports Science Assoc., 1984.

Mobility Training, N. Brook, B.A.A.B., 1990.

Peak Performance, R.N. Singer, Movement Pubs. Inc., 1986.

Perfecting Pole Vault Technique, N. Houvion, 1984.

Safety First in Pole Vaulting, P.B. Sutcliffe, The Jumper, 1988.

Sporting Body Sporting Mind, J. Syer and C. Connolly, Simon & Schuster, 1987.

Training Theory, F.W. Dick, B.A.A.B., 1984.

The Vault System, R. Bussabarger, 1985.

APPENDIX 1
OLYMPIC CHAMPIONS; EVOLUTION OF UK AND WORLD RECORDS

OLYMPIC POLE VAULT CHAMPIONS

Year	Athlete	Country	Height
1896	William Hoyt	USA	3.30 m
1900	Irving Baxter	USA	3.30 m
1904	Charles Dvorak	USA	3.50 m
1906	Fernand Gonder	France	3.40 m
1908	Edward Cooke	USA	3.70 m
	Alfred Gilbert	USA	3.70 m
1912	Harry Babcock	USA	3.95 m
1920	Frank Foss	USA	4.09 m
1924	Lee Barnes	USA	3.95 m
1928	Sabin Carr	USA	4.20 m
1932	William Miller	USA	4.31 m
1936	Earle Meadows	USA	4.35 m
1948	Guinn Smith	USA	4.30 m
1952	Bob Richards	USA	4.55 m
1956	Bob Richards	USA	4.56 m
1960	Don Bragg	USA	4.70 m
1964	Fred Hansen	USA	5.10 m
1968	Bob Seagren	USA	5.40 m
1972	Wolfgang Nordwig	GDR	5.50 m
1976	Tadeusz Slusarki	POL	5.50 m
1980	Wladislaw Kozakiewicz	POL	5.78 m
1984	Pierre Quinon	FRA	5.75 m
1988	Sergei Bubka	URS	5.90 m

EVOLUTION OF UK POLE VAULT RECORD

Date	Athlete	Height
28/08/54	Geoff Elliott	4.30 m
22/06/63	Rex Porter	4.32 m
05/08/63	Trevor Burton	4.37 m
30/08/63	Rex Porter	4.39 m
14/09/63	David Stevenson	4.40 m
21/09/63	David Stevenson	4.41 m
25/09/63	David Stevenson	4.42 m
16/05/64	Trevor Burton	4.43 m
20/06/64	Trevor Burton	4.46 m
11/07/64	Trevor Burton	4.57 m
25/07/64	David Stevenson	4.60 m
29/08/64	David Stevenson	4.61 m

EVOLUTION OF UK POLE VAULT RECORD continued

Date	Athlete	Height
25/05/66	David Stevenson	4.65 m
28/05/66	David Stevenson	4.67 m
13/09/66	Mike Bull	4.72 m
02/09/67	Mike Bull	4.80 m
26/06/68	Mike Bull	4.94 m
12/09/68	Mike Bull	5.03 m
14/09/68	Mike Bull	5.07 m
23/07/70	Mike Bull	5.10 m
04/06/72	Mike Bull	5.11 m
21/06/72	Mike Bull	5.20 m
15/07/72	Mike Bull	5.21 m
22/09/73	Mike Bull	5.25 m
19/04/76	Brian Hooper	5.29 m
14/05/76	Brian Hooper	5.30 m
07/08/76	Brian Hooper	5.31 m
22/08/76	Brian Hooper	5.32 m
30/07/77	Brian Hooper	5.37 m
29/08/77	Brian Hooper	5.40 m
19/08/78	Brian Hooper	5.41 m
17/09/78	Brian Hooper	5.42 m
08/08/80	Brian Hooper	5.45 m
16/08/80	Brian Hooper	5.50 m
20/08/80	Brian Hooper	5.51 m
06/09/80	Keith Stock	5.52 m
06/09/80	Brian Hooper	5.54 m
06/09/80	Keith Stock	5.55 m
06/09/80	Brian Hooper	5.56 m
06/09/80	Keith Stock	5.57 m
06/09/80	Brian Hooper	5.58 m
06/09/80	Brian Hooper	5.59 m
07/07/81	Keith Stock	5.65 m

EVOLUTION OF WORLD POLE VAULT RECORD
(Outdoor Marks Only)

Year	Athlete	Country	Height
1940	Cornelius Warmerdam	USA	4.57 m (15 ft)
1944	Cornelius Warmerdam	USA	4.77 m
1957	Bob Gutowski	USA	4.82 m
1961	George Davies	USA	4.83 m
1962	John Uelsis	USA	4.89 m (16 ft)
1962	Dave Tork	USA	4.93 m
1962	Pentti Nikula	FIN	4.94 m
1963	John Pennel	USA	4.95 m

EVOLUTION OF WORLD POLE VAULT RECORD continued
(Outdoor Marks Only)

Year	Athlete	Country	Height
1963	John Pennel	USA	4.98 m
1963	Brian Sternberg	USA	5.00 m
1963	John Pennel	USA	5.05 m
1963	Brian Sternberg	USA	5.08 m
1963	John Pennel	USA	5.10 m
1963	John Pennel	USA	5.13 m
1963	John Pennel	USA	5.20 m (17 ft)
1964	Fred Hansen	USA	5.23 m
1964	Fred Hansen	USA	5.28 m
1966	Bob Seagren	USA	5.32 m
1966	John Pennel	USA	5.34 m
1967	Bob Seagren	USA	5.36 m
1967	Paul Wilson	USA	5.38 m
1968	Bob Seagren	USA	5.41 m
1969	John Pennel	USA	5.44 m
1970	Wolfgang Nordwig	GDR	5.45 m
1970	Wolfgang Nordwig	GDR	5.46 m
1970	Christos Papanicolaou	GRE	5.48 m (18 ft)
1972	Kjell Isaksson	SWE	5.51 m
1972	Kjell Isaksson	SWE	5.54 m
1972	Bob Seagren	USA	5.63 m
1975	Dave Roberts	USA	5.65 m
1976	Earl Bell	USA	5.67 m
1976	Dave Roberts	USA	5.70 m
1980	Wladyslaw Kozakiewicz	POL	5.72 m
1980	Thierry Vigneron	FRA	5.75 m
1980	Phillipe Houvion	FRA	5.77 m
1980	Wladyslaw Kozakiewicz	POL	5.78 m (19 ft)
1981	Vladimir Polyakov	URS	5.81 m
1983	Thierry Vigneron	FRA	5.83 m
1984	Sergei Bubka	URS	5.90 m
1984	Sergei Bubka	URS	5.94 m
1985	Sergei Bubka	URS	6.00 m
1986	Sergei Bubka	URS	6.01 m
1987	Sergei Bubka	URS	6.03 m
1988	Sergei Bubka	URS	6.06 m

APPENDIX 2
VAULT SEQUENCES

Billy Olsen (U.S.A.)

Rodion Gataullin (U.S.S.R.)

Alexander Krupski (U.S.S.R.)

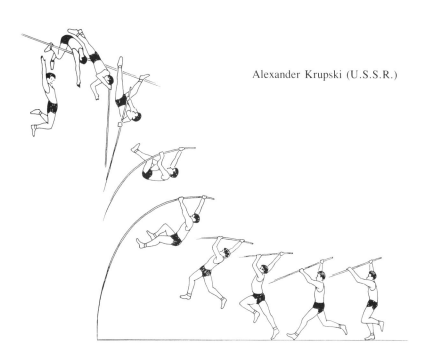

APPENDIX 3
PHOTO
SEQUENCE
OF
THIERRY
VIGNERON
(FRANCE)

APPENDIX 4
SAMPLE PROGRAMMES

The following schedules represent guidelines only. Programmes should be drawn up bearing in mind the needs of each individual athlete.

Sample Programme for Young Beginner

Week

Monday	—
Tuesday	— Slow Steady Run : Circuit Exercises
Wednesday	—
Thursday	— Vault : Drills
Friday	—
Saturday	—
Sunday	— Vault : Drills : Circuit Exercises

1. Mobility and skipping to be done at home.
2. Circuit exercises are bodyweight with particular attention to abdominal and dorsal muscles.
3. Drills are primarily plant and approach drills.

Sample programme October-January for vaulter aged 15-16 years vaulting approximately 4.30 m.

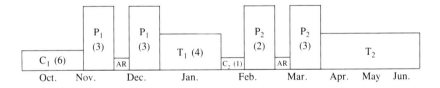

Oct.	Nov.	Dec.	Jan.	Feb.	Mar.	Apr.	May	Jun.	

C_1 (6) P_1 (3) P_1 (3) AR T_1 (4) C_2 (1) P_2 (2) AR P_2 (3) T_2

C_1 Conditioning — 6 weeks

Monday	— Gymnastics
Tuesday	— Rest
Wednesday	— Vault Skipping Circuit
Thursday	— Steady run 3-4 miles
Friday	— Rest
Saturday	— Fartlek or Games
Sunday	— Vault Circuit

P_1 Preparation 1-2 × 3 weeks

Monday	— Gymnastics
Tuesday	— Rest

Wednesday — Vault   Circuit
Thursday — Track (2 × 5 × 80m. at 70%; walk back recovery
            between reps.; 3 mins. between sets; 10 mins.
            between series).   Drills
Friday   — Rest
Saturday — Games
Sunday   — Vault   Circuit

T₁ Technical Period — 4 weeks

Monday   — Gymnastics
Tuesday   — Drills
Wednesday — Vault   Drills   Circuit
Thursday — Rest   Drills
Friday   — Rest
Saturday — Competition or Rest
Sunday   — Vault   Drills   Circuit

AR   Active Rest   Games

Sample programme for senior vaulter vaulting approximately 5.00 m.

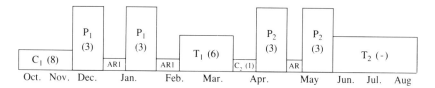

C₁ Conditioning I — 8 weeks

Week 1

Monday   — Jogging ¾-1 mile
Tuesday   —
Wednesday — General weights
Thursday —
Friday   —
Saturday — Jogging ¾-1 mile
Sunday   — Gymnastics

Weeks 2/3

Monday   — Jogging 1-1½ miles + circuit
Tuesday   —
Wednesday — Weights
Thursday — Gymnastics
Friday   — Weights
Saturday — Jogging 1½ miles
Sunday   — Skipping 45 secs. + circuit

87

Weeks 4/5

Monday — Steady run 2-2½ miles   Weights
Tuesday — Skipping 1 min.   Circuit
Wednesday — Weights
Thursday — Pole vault drills   Track (2 × 400 m. easy ;
6 × 100 m. easy)
Friday — Rest
Saturday — Weights
Sunday — Fartlek   Circuit

Week 6

Monday — Steady run 3 miles   Weights
Tuesday — Skipping 1 min.   Hopping (2 × 30 m.)   Circuit
Wednesday — Weights
Thursday — Running   Drill   Circuit
Friday — Rest
Saturday — Weights
Track (2 × 400 m. easy; 6 × 100 m. easy)
Sunday — Fartlek   Circuit

Weeks 7/8

Monday — Hill run   Weights
Tuesday — Plyometrics (1)   Circuit
Wednesday — Track (3 × 300 m.; 4 × 100 m. 70% 2-3 mins. rec.)
Weights
Thursday — Pole vault drills   Skipping 2 mins.   Circuit
Friday — Rest
Saturday — Pole vault drills   Weights
Sunday — Fartlek

Weights

Circuits: 3-5; Exercises: 6; Sets: 3; Repetitions: 20-30; Resistance: 30%-40%. 1RM; Speed: Brisk tempo; Recovery: 60 secs. between sets, 3 mins. between circuits.

Plyometrics

2 × Hop 20 m. on right leg and bound back 20 m. to start and hop 20 m. on left leg and bound back 20 m. to start and double leg jump to 20 m. and sprint back to start. (5-8 mins. recovery between sets.)

Fartlek

Jog 5-10 mins., run ¾-1¼ miles at fast steady pace, walk 5 mins., alternate jog sprints (30 m.) for 2 mins., sprint uphill 100-150 m., jog ¾-1¼ miles.

Drills

Running drills
Acceleration runs with plant
When fully fit — vaults into sand

Circuits

Maximum repetitions in 60 secs.

A.	B.	C.
Press-ups	Dips	Jumps against wall
Sit-ups	Tuck jumps	Hyperextensions
Hyperextensions	Shuttle runs	(on floor)
(on floor)	Medicine ball throws	Stride jumps
$\frac{1}{2}$ squats	(chest)	Press-ups
V-sits	Burpees	Chinnies
Squat thrusts	Chinnies	Step-ups
Pillars	Hyperextensions	V-sits
Tuck jumps	(on floor)	Squat thrusts
	V-sits	

P₁ Preparation 1 (2 × 3 weeks)

Monday — Weights
Tuesday — Short approach vaults   Plyometrics
Wednesday — Track 3 × 150 m., 6 × 100 m. 70%   2-3 mins. rec.
Weights
Thursday — Short approach vaults   Plyometrics   Circuit
Friday — Weights
Saturday — Rest
Sunday — Gymnastics   Drills   Body Tension Circuit

Weights

Set 1: 8 at 70% 1RM; Set 2: 7 at 85% 1RM; Set 3: 2 at 95% 1RM; Set 4: 6 secs. at 90% 1RM; Set 5: 6 secs. at 90% 1RM; Set 6: 5 at 85% 1RM; Set 7: 5 at 85% 1RM. Recovery: 2 mins. after sets 1, 2, 6; 4 mins. after sets 3, 4, 5.

Plyometrics

1. (3 weeks) bounding 2 × 5 × 30 m.

    3-5 stride approach 1-2 mins. recovery between repetitions.
    8 mins. recovery between sets with light running and stretching

2. (3 weeks) bounding 3 × 5 × 30 m.

Circuits 2 × maximum 60 secs.

A.	B.

A.

$\frac{1}{2}$ squats
Press-ups (push off ground/bench)
Hyperextensions (on bench with
   medicine ball)
Sit-ups with pole
Medicine ball throws overhead
Jumps against wall
V-sits

B.

Tuck jumps
Leg raises
Hyperextensions
Chinnies
V-sits
Step-ups
Chinnies

AR — Active Rest

Break from athletics/games.

Technical Period I (6 weeks)

Monday	— Track (4×100, 6×60 90%, full recovery)	Circuit
Tuesday	— Games	
Wednesday	— Gymnastics Games	
Thursday	— Vaulting Drills	
Friday	—	
Saturday	— Gymnastics Games	
Sunday	— Vaulting Drills Circuit	

Circuit

Rope climbs
Rock backs on rope
Medicine ball throws (overhead and from chest)
Muscle-ups
Hyperextensions
Rock back and extension through pole
Sit-ups with pole
Shuttle runs

Conditioning 2 (1 week) as for week 8 in C_1.

P_2 Preparation 2 (2×3 weeks) as for P_1 (10% increased loading)

Bo1 & T_2 (variable)

Monday	— Track (6×60, 6×90 m. 100%, full recovery)
Tuesday	— Rest
Wednesday	— Weights
Thursday	— Vaults Drills
Friday	— Rest
Saturday	— Competition
Sunday	— Vault/drills Circuit

* Mobility every day throughout the year.

90

Sample programme for experienced international

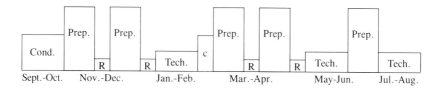

	Prep.	Prep.		Prep.	Prep.		Prep.
Cond.			c				
	R	R Tech.		R	R Tech.		Tech.
Sept.-Oct.	Nov.-Dec.	Jan.-Feb.		Mar.-Apr.		May-Jun.	Jul.-Aug.

1. Preparation Periods: 2 × 4 weekly cycles — 3 weeks complex training, 1 week recuperation.
2. Technical Periods: Technique work or competition.
3. Complete physical and medical checks after preparation periods.

Conditioning — 8 weeks
Week 1

Monday	—	Active recovery
Tuesday	—	Slow running (4 miles 7 mins. per mile)
Wednesday	—	Weights
Thursday	—	Active rest
Friday	—	Slow running (as above)
Saturday	—	Weights
Sunday	—	Skipping (3 × 2 mins)

Week 2

Monday	—	Weights Slow running (as above)
Tuesday	—	Circuit exercises
Wednesday	—	Weights
Thursday	—	Active recovery
Friday	—	Weights
Saturday	—	Fartlek
Sunday	—	Running 4 × 200 m. (easy) 6 × 100 m. (easy)

Week 3

Monday	—	Weights Slow running (5 miles)
Tuesday	—	Circuit Pole vault drills
Wednesday	—	Weights
Thursday	—	Active recovery
Friday	—	Weights
Saturday	—	Fartlek Circuit
Sunday	—	Pole vault drills Running 2 × 400 m. (easy) 6 × 100 m. (easy)

Week 4

Monday   — Weights   Slow running (5 miles)
Tuesday   — Running 1 × 800 m. (easy) 6 × 200 m. (easy)   Circuit
Wednesday — Weights
Thursday   — Active recovery
Friday   — Gymnastics
Saturday   — Fartlek   Games
Sunday   — Pole vault drills   Circuit

Week 5

Monday   — Weights   Hill runs
Tuesday   — Skipping and hopping (2 × 50 m.)   Circuit
Wednesday — Weights
Thursday   — Pole vault drills   Circuit
Friday   — Gymnastics
Saturday   — Fartlek   Circuit
Sunday   — Pole vault drills   Running 2 × 400 m. (easy)
                6 × 100 m. (easy)

Week 6

Monday   — Weights   Hill runs
Tuesday   — Skipping and hopping (2 × 60 m.)   Circuit
Wednesday — Weights   Running 3 × 300 m., 4 × 100 m.
                70% (3 mins. recovery)
Thursday   — Active recovery
Friday   — Gymnastics
Saturday   — Fartlek
Sunday   — Short approach vaults   Pole vault drills

Week 7

Monday   — Weights   Hill runs
Tuesday   — Bounding (2 × 50 m.)   Circuit
Wednesday — Weights   Running 5 × 100 m., 8 × 60 m. 70%
Thursday   — Pole vault drills   Circuit
Friday   — Gymnastics
Saturday   — Fartlek
Sunday   — Short approach vaults   Pole vault drills

Week 8

Monday   — Weights   Hill run
Tuesday   — Bounding (2 × 60 m.)   Circuit
Wednesday — Weights   Running 4 × 150 m., 6 × 100 m. 70%
Thursday   — Short approach vaults   Pole vault drills and circuit
Friday   — Gymnastics
Saturday   — Fartlek
Sunday   — Tests

Weights

Weeks 1-2   Bench press   Lateral pull-ups
              Inclined sit-up   Curls
              Inclined bench press   Cleans

Circuits: 5-6; Sets: 3; Repetitions: 30; Resistance: 40% 1RM; Speed: Brisk tempo; Recovery: 60 secs. between sets, 3 mins. between circuits.

Weeks 3-8   Leg press   Bench press
              Leg curls   Partial snatch
              Sit-up   Arm curl

Circuits: 3; Sets: 5-6; Repetitions: Max. in 30 secs.; Resistance: 50%-60% 1RM; Speed: Explosive: Recovery: 15 secs. between sets, 90 secs. between circuits.

Fartlek

Jog 5-10 mins.; run 1-2 miles at fast steady pace; walk 5 mins.; alternate jog-sprint 50 m. for $1\frac{1}{2}$ mins.; sprint uphill 100 m.; jog 1 mile.

Pole vault drills

Pop-ups
Vaults into sand
High knees
Plants into moveable box
Acceleration runs with pole and plant
Runs over sticks with pole
Fast feet.

Circuits

A.	B.
Hand-stand press-up	Rock-back on wall bars
$\frac{1}{2}$ squats	Rock-back + extension through pole
Rock-back + extension through pole	Speed climb on rope
Hyperextension with pole	Upside down on rope
Chinnies	Rock-back on rope
V-sits	Muscle-ups
Muscle-ups	Medicine ball throws
Wall jumps	Hyperextensions

C.

Sit-ups
Handstand press-ups
Wall jumps
Crunchees with pole
Rock-back + extension with pole
Hyperextensions with pole
Burpees
V-sits

D.

Hand-stand press-ups
Rock-back + extension through
  pole
Crunchees with pole
V-sits
Hyperextensions with pole
Chinnies
Basketball throws against wall
Wall jumps

E.

Rock-back
Hyperextensions with pole
V-sits
Squat jumps
Press-ups clapping hands
Rock-back + extension through
  pole
Sit-ups
Wall jumps

F.

Split calf jumps
Press-ups clapping hands
Sit-ups with pole
Tuck jumps
Chinnies
Burpees
Hyperextensions with pole
Leg raises on wall bars

Preparation 1

Week 1

Monday	— Complex 1
Tuesday	— Complex 2
Wednesday	— Complex 3 + Abdominal/dorsal circuit
Thursday	— Complex 4 + Short approach vaults
Friday	— Gymnastics
Saturday	— Complex 5 + Abdominal/dorsal circuit
Sunday	— Short approach vaults Running drills

Week 2

Monday	— Complex 6
Tuesday	— Complex 7
Wednesday	— Complex 8 + Circuit
Thursday	— Complex 4 + Short approach vaults
Friday	— Gymnastics
Saturday	— Complex 9 + Circuit
Sunday	— Short approach vaults Running drills

Week 3

Monday	— Complex 6
Tuesday	— Complex 2

Wednesday — Complex 10 + Circuit
Thursday — Complex 4 + Short approach vaults
Friday — Gymnastics
Saturday — Complex 9 + Circuit
Sunday — Short approach vaults   Running drills

Week 4

Monday — Rest
Tuesday — Games
Wednesday — Games
Thursday — Rest
Friday — Rest
Saturday — Games
Sunday — Rest

To be repeated over next four weeks.

Complexes

1. Bench press: 2 × 2-3 reps. 90% 1 RM
   3-4 mins. between sets
   4-6 mins. after both sets
   Medicine ball throws 2 × 10
   3-4 mins. between sets
   Repeat twice with 8-10 mins. between complexes.

2. $\frac{1}{2}$ squats: 1 × 2-3 reps. 90% 1 RM
   rest 4-6 mins.
   $\frac{1}{2}$ squats: 2 × 2 × 6-8 reps. 30% 1 RM
   rest 3-4 mins. between sets
       4-6 mins. after sets
   Alternate leg bounding 5 jumps off each leg 2 × 5 reps. (5 jumps off
     each leg = 1 rep.)
   rest 1 min. between reps.
       3-4 mins between sets
       4-6 mins. after sets
   Acceleration sprints: 3-4 × 50 m.
   rest 15 secs. between sprints
   Repeat twice with 6-8 mins. between complexes.

3. Inclined press + medicine ball (as Complex 1).

4. Calf raises + jumps over hurdles (2 × 6 over 4 hurdles).

5. $\frac{1}{2}$ squats + jumps over hurdles.

6. Medicine ball throws 2 × 20 + basketball rebounds 2 × 20.

7. $\frac{1}{2}$ squats + sequence of 5 standing long jumps.

8. Curls + muscle-ups.

9. Cleans + bounding (2 × 40 m.).

10. Bench press + basketball against wall (2 × 45 secs.).

Technical Period 1 (6 weeks)

Monday   —
Tuesday   — Full approach vaults: 3 × 5 × 60 m. Full recovery
Wednesday — Games
Thursday   — Drills   Full recovery sprints   Body tension circuit
Friday   — Rest
Saturday   — Competition or games
Sunday   — Full approach vaults (if no competition on Saturday)
                Drills   Circuit

Preparation 2

As for Preparation 1 but:

(a) 3 complexes per session.

(b) 10% extra loading.

(c) Complexes 5 and 7 substitute depth jumps 2 × 10 (height .75 m.).

(d) Introduce snatch into complex programme.

Note: Mobility sessions 3-4 × per week.

TALENT TEST FOR POLE VAULT

Age	30 m. sprint	60 m. sprint	Standing long jump	Long jump with run	Push-ups	4 m. rope climb	Vertical jump	Rope swing over bar	Evaluation
11	5.4	9.2	1.80	4.60	12	10.5	40		Below average
to	5.2	9.0	2.00	4.80	15	10.0	45		Average
12	5.0	8.8	2.10	5.00	18	9.5	51		Good
13	4.6	8.4	2.20	5.00	18	9.0	50		Below average
to	4.5	8.2	2.30	5.15	22	8.5	55		Average
14	4.4	8.0	2.40	5.30	25	8.0	60		Good

Age: ....

Name: ....

Address: ....

School/Club.......................................

Date of Birth: ....

Weight: ....

Height: ....

Arm Length: ....

97

COACHES REPORT SHEET

Date: ....

Meeting: ....

Venue: ....

Name: ....

Nationality: ....

Length of run used: ....

Time over last 6 strides: ....

Pole used: ....

Grip: .... Push off: ....

Height Achieved: ....

Position of stands: ....

Condition of the runway: ....

Condition of the landing area: ....

Weather conditions: ....

Temperature: .... Sunny / Cloudy / Wet

Wind: Strength: ....

        Direction: ....

Technique: ....

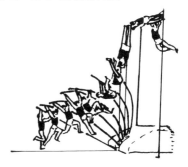

ATHLETICS PUBLICATIONS

INSTRUCTIONAL BOOKS
for athletes and officials

OFFICIAL HANDBOOKS

SCORING TABLES

COACHING MANUALS, ETC

For an up-to-date price list please
send s.a.e. to:

**Athletics Publications Sales Centre,
5 Church Road,
Great Bookham,
Surrey KT23 3PN**

Telephone:
Bookham (03724) 52804